UCHICAGO **Consortium**
on School Research

RESEARCH BRIEF   JUNE 2024

Removing Police Officers from Chicago Schools

Trends and Outcomes

Amy Arneson, Rebecca Hinze-Pifer, Kaitlyn Franklin, David W. Johnson

TABLE OF CONTENTS

ACKNOWLEDGEMENTS

The authors gratefully acknowledge the district and community partners who have been, and continue to be, engaged in this research. We would like to thank the staff at Chicago Public Schools Offices of School Safety and Security and Social and Emotional Learning, particularly Jadine Chou, Kylie Kosmacek, Maria Venegas, and Benjamin McKay, for their insight and championing of this work. We appreciate the enthusiastic engagement of the Whole School Safety Steering Committee in the research process: Broader Urban Involvement & Leadership Development (BUILD), Community Organizing and Family Issues (COFI), Mikva Challenge, and Voices of Youth in Chicago Education (VOYCE). Thank you to Charlene Campbell, Maria Degillo, Davarius Jones, Kandace Mack, Aida Palma Carpio, Delia Perez, Sean Price, Carla Rubalcava, Romya Simone, Arianna Tello, and your youth and parent partners for sharing your expertise and welcoming us into your community. We are grateful to Rodney Thomas of Center Forward and Alex Fralin of Leading Partnerships for their planning and facilitation work that has supported and enhanced these partnerships.

In addition, we thank Elaine Allensworth, Bronwyn McDaniel, Jessica Tansey, Chen An, and Jenny Nagaoka for thorough and thoughtful feedback on our drafts, Jessica Puller for careful editing, and Julia Gwynne and Chris Young for detailed technical reviews. Thank you especially to Lucy Sorensen for guidance in the project design and ongoing support in meaning making. Any errors or omissions are the sole responsibility of the authors.

This research brief was supported by the Pritzker-Pucker Family Foundation, the W. Clement and Jessie V. Stone Foundation, Crown Family Philanthropies, and the Consortium Investor Council which funds critical work at the Consortium: putting the research to work, refreshing the data archive, seeding new studies, and replicating previous studies. Consortium Investor Council members include: Brinson Foundation, CME Group Foundation, Crown Family Philanthropies, Lloyd A. Fry Foundation, Joyce Foundation, Lewis-Sebring Family Foundation, Mayer & Morris Kaplan Family Foundation, Robert R. McCormick Foundation, McDougal Family Foundation, Polk Bros. Foundation, Spencer Foundation, Steans Family Foundation, Square One Foundation, The Chicago Public Education Fund, the Vivo Foundation, and two anonymous foundations. The UChicago Consortium thanks the Lewis-Sebring Family Foundation, whose operating grant supports our work.

Cite as: Arneson, A., Hinze-Pifer, R., Franklin, K., & Johnson, D.W. (2024). *Removing police officers from Chicago schools: Trends and outcomes.* Chicago, IL: University of Chicago Consortium on School Research.

This report was produced by the UChicago Consortium's publications and communications staff: Jessica Tansey, Managing Director of Research Communications: Bronwyn McDaniel, Communications Manager; and Jessica Puller, Senior Communications Strategist.

Graphic Design: Jeff Hall Design
Photography: Eileen Ryan
Editing: Bronwyn McDaniel, Jessica Tansey, and Jessica Puller

---

06.2024/PDF/jh.design@rcn.com

Introduction

Schools across the United States have long grappled with the role and impact of school-based police officers, often referred to as school resource officers (SROs).[1] Proponents for school-based policing believe that SROs contribute to school safety by preventing or addressing crime and violence in schools. Opponents of SROs in schools argue that the presence of SROs criminalizes students and increases the likelihood of school-based arrest, particularly for students of color. Policies around SROs vary in districts across the country.

These debates became more urgent in the wake of the murder of George Floyd in 2020, leading school communities across the country to interrogate the presence of SROs in schools and remove SROs in some places.[2] In Chicago, the Board of Education asked the district to develop a plan to phase-out the SRO program, which assigned two SROs to most CPS high schools.[3] As part of this effort, Chicago Public Schools (CPS) partnered with a group of community-based organizations (CBOs) to develop the Whole School Safety (WSS) Framework which defines school safety holistically with three pillars of **1) physical safety, 2) emotional safety, and 3) relational trust.** Schools then established Whole School Safety committees comprised of members of the school community to reflect on the proactive and reactive measures used in the school to support students' physical safety, emotional safety, and relational trust and develop WSS Plans. Additionally, the Board gave decision-making power to Local School Councils (LSCs)[4] about whether SROs remained on high school

campuses and the first LSC votes were held in summer 2020. Starting in the 2021–22 school year, schools that removed SROs were offered compensatory funding to reinvest in other safety-related activities in the school.

These choices were made against a backdrop of existing research that provides mixed evidence regarding the impact of police presence in schools. Studies broadly find SROs increase reported behavioral infractions and suspensions, particularly for students of color, or have no impact on these outcomes.[5] Researchers note that it is impossible to determine whether these changes arise from differences in underlying student behavior or differences in detection and/or reporting of that behavior. Most studies do not examine how SROs[6] affect perceptions of school safety by students and teachers, although a few find educators believe safety is improved or unchanged with SROs, with either no impact or a worsening of perceived safety among students.[7] In studies that interview students directly (typically in focus groups), students express a range of

---

1   In data collected by the U.S. Department of Education for the 2017–18 school year (the most recent available), 53% of high schools reported a full-time SRO on campus and another 21% reported an SRO on campus at least once a week (Wang, Kemp & Burr, 2022). There is some evidence this data underestimates SRO presence (Curran & Boza, 2023).
2   Riser-Kositsky, Sawchuk, & Peele (2021, June 4).
3   There were no SROs in CPS elementary or K-8 schools at the time.

4   Local School Councils are the elected governing bodies in Chicago that make decisions about principal hiring and other school-level policies.
5   Fisher & Hennessy (2016); Gottfredson et al. (2020); Owens (2017); Sorensen, Avila-Acosta, Engberg, & Bushway (2023); Weisburst (2019); Zhang (2019).
6   Chrusciel, Wolfe, Hansen, Rojek, & Kaminski (2015); Kurtz (2020, June 26); Wolfe, Chrusciel, Rojek, Hansen, & Kaminski (2017).

perspectives from feeling distrustful and criminalized by SROs, to ambivalence about SRO presence, to feeling protected and supported by SROs.[8]

This brief describes the initial findings from a study of the changes in SRO presence in CPS. The central questions that we explored are:

1. What were the characteristics of schools that retained, partially removed, or fully removed SROs?

   - What were the characteristics of students in schools that made different decisions about SROs?

2. When CPS high schools removed one or both SROs, how did school climate (student and teacher perceptions of physical safety, student perceptions of relationships with teachers) and discipline outcomes (infractions, high-level infractions, suspensions, and police notifications) change?

We investigated the first question descriptively using CPS administrative data on district-run high schools and the ninth- through twelfth-grade students enrolled in them from 2014–15 through 2022–23. Schools were placed into four categories based on their SRO status in 2022–23—**1) Retained both (2 SROs), 2) Partially Removed (1 SRO), 3) Fully Removed (0 SROs), and 4) None at Baseline (0 SROs)**—and we compared student characteristics (race/ethnicity, gender, free and reduced-price lunch eligibility, English Learner status, and special education status) and school characteristics (populations served, school size, and suspension rates) within each group. We found variation in most of these characteristics among the different categories of SRO presence. In particular, we found notable differences by race/ethnicity in terms of the student populations experiencing different levels of SRO presence in their schools.

For the second question, we employed a difference-in-difference approach, comparing school climate and discipline outcomes from school year 2018–19 (prior to the Board of Education resolution) to 2022–23 (the most current year available) using CPS administrative and survey data. This method accounts for changes in the school climate and discipline outcomes over the study period, and provides an estimate of the difference in the change of an outcome among the different SRO status categories.[9] We examined outcomes at the school-level (e.g., annual counts of discipline infractions, high-level discipline infractions, suspensions, police notifications, and school-level scores of Student Physical Safety, Teacher Physical Safety, and Student-Teacher Trust) and at the individual student-level (e.g., odds of having a reported infraction, high-level infraction, suspension, police notification, and student-level scores of Student Physical Safety and Student-Teacher Trust).

Overall, we found that when SROs were removed from CPS high schools, there were statistically significant reductions in reported high-level behavioral infractions [10] within schools and in the chances that a student has a high-level behavioral infraction. For police notifications, though the school-level result was not statistically significant, the reduction in notifications may be substantive in a practical sense. We did not detect statistically significant changes on infractions overall or suspensions. We also examined measures from the *5Essentials* survey most closely aligned to the WSS Framework. Student and teacher perceptions of physical safety—which we will refer to as "Student Physical Safety" and "Teacher Physical Safety" for the remainder of this brief—and Student-Teacher Trust, a component of relational trust, did not significantly

7   Curran, Viano, Kupchik, & Fisher (2021); Javdani (2019); Theriot (2016); Theriot & Orme (2016).

8   E.g., Cobbina, Galasso, Cunningham, Melde, & Heinze (2020); Layton & Gerstenblatt (2022).

9   Difference-in-difference analysis is often used to estimate a causal effect. We do not feel that the assumptions required for a causal interpretation are met in this analysis, so we cannot attribute any observed changes solely to the removal or retention of SROs in CPS high schools. One of our chief concerns is the possible differential impact of the COVID-19 pandemic on schools that made different decisions about SROs. However, the difference-in-difference and covariate adjustments still provide important information about school climate and discipline outcomes prior to and after the removal of SROs. This is discussed further in Appendix C.

10 The CPS Student Code of Conduct categorizes behaviors into six levels. For this study, high-level discipline infractions are the three most severe categories: 1) "very seriously disrupt," 2) "most seriously disrupt," and 3) "are illegal and most seriously disrupt." These include most violent incidents, serious threats of violence, and all alcohol, drug, and weapons-related infractions. https://www.cps.edu/about/policies/student-code-of-conduct-policy/

change at either the school or student levels.[11]

Table 1 contains the summary of findings for each of the outcomes examined in this brief, along with the items on each of the survey measures.

We chose the *5Essentials* Survey and other annual survey outcomes that are most closely related to the pillars of the WSS Framework. The Student and Teacher Physical Safety measures capture elements of the

physical safety pillar of the WSS Framework. The Student-Teacher Trust measure reflects a portion of the relational trust pillar, but we acknowledge that neither was designed to be aligned with the other and the SRO program was not intended to address relationships between students and teachers. However, we feel it is a relevant outcome to examine as the WSS Framework calls for increased attention to school climate and,

TABLE 1

Summary of high school outcome analyses

Outcome	After the removal of SROs, was there a change in…	…at the school-level?	…at the student-level?
Discipline	Discipline infractions	Not significantly	Not significantly
	High-level discipline infractions	**Yes, a reduction**	**Yes, a reduction**
	Suspensions (in-school and out-of-school)	Not significantly	Not significantly
	Police notifications	**A potentially meaningful reduction, but not statistically significant**	Not significantly
School Climate	**Student Physical Safety** How safe do you feel? - In the hallways of the school. - In the bathrooms of the school. - Outside around the school. - Traveling between home and school. - In your classes.	Not significantly	Not significantly
	Teacher Physical Safety To what extent is each of the following a problem at your school: - Physical conflicts among students - Robbery or theft - Gang activity - Disorder in classrooms - Disorder in hallways - Student disrespect of teachers - Threats of violence towards teachers	Not significantly	N/A
	Student-Teacher Trust How much do you disagree or agree with the following statements? - I feel safe with my teachers at this school. - I feel comfortable with my teachers at this school. - My teachers always keep their promises. - My teachers always listen to students' ideas. - My teachers treat me with respect.	Not significantly	Not significantly

Note: We flag results that were statistically significant at the alpha = 0.10 level.

---

11 The School Safety (referred to as "Student Physical Safety") and Student-Teacher Trust student measures are validated measures from the *5Essentials* Survey (Hart, Young, Chen, Zou, & Allensworth, 2020). The Teacher Safety (referred to as "Teacher Physical Safety") measure is administered at the same time, annually, as a supplement to the *5Essentials* Survey, though it is not directly aligned to the *5Essentials* framework. The School Safety and Teacher Safety measures focus on aspects of physical safety, so we refer to these as "Student Physical Safety" and "Teacher Physical Safety" in this brief in order to differentiate them from the other pillars of school safety as defined by the WSS Framework.

specifically, relational trust among members of the school community. While we may not expect to see dramatic changes in distal school climate outcomes immediately after SRO removal, this work provides an initial look and a structure for examining such outcomes in the future. Details on the survey measures and all other variables, including the outcomes, are provided in **Appendix A**.

Districtwide data and trends

At the time of the 2020 Board resolution that established LSCs as the decision makers on the presence of SROs in high schools, there were 84 district-run high school campuses in CPS; 13 of them had removed SROs prior to 2020 while the rest had the "status quo" of two SROs stationed at their campuses.[12] Starting in the 2020–21 school year, the number of SROs across the district began to decline as LSC votes fully removed SROs at their schools, partially removed SROs, or retained both. Figure 1 shows the changes in SRO counts across CPS high school campuses. In the most recent school year, 2023–24, 39 campuses had at least one SRO (17 retained both and 22 partially removed SROs) and 44 campuses had no SROs (inclusive of the 13 that had none at baseline).

In order to retain SROs or receive funding to reinvest in alternate safety-oriented activities if SROs were removed, high schools were required to assemble a WSS Committee and participate in WSS planning, a process that was co-designed with five community-based organizations[13] that had advocated for police removal and who had worked with CPS to develop the WSS Framework.[14] Almost all schools that used SRO reinvestment funds spent them on staffing in one of

The number of CPS high school campuses with SROs began declining in the 2020–21 school year

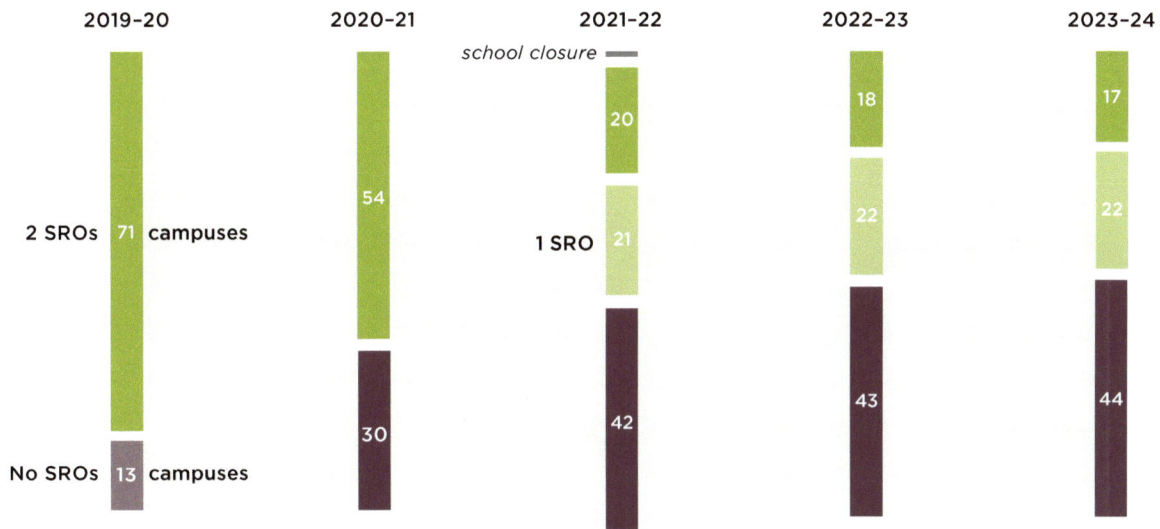

Note: For 2020–21, LSCs voted on whether to retain or remove the SRO program in total. The option of partial removal was first available for 2021–22. This figure shows the number of district-run high school campuses (or sites) with two, one, or zero SROs during each school year from 2019-20 through 2023-24. There were two campuses with co-located high schools (one with two high schools and one with four high schools). Co-located schools shared their SROs and jointly made the decision about whether to retain SROs. In addition, one high school had two separate campuses, each with two SROs. Other analyses in this brief are conducted at the school-level, so total counts of units or clusters may differ for this reason.

12 No CPS elementary or K-8 schools had SROs in any year discussed. Charter, Options (alternative), virtual, and special education school schools are not included as they were not subject to the same policies related to SROs. One charter school did have SROs on campus during the study period, but is not included in any analysis as data on charter schools' discipline outcomes are not collected by the district.

13 The ARK of St. Sabina, Broader Urban Involvement & Leadership Development (BUILD), Community Organizing and Family Issues (COFI), Mikva Challenge, and Voices of Youth in Chicago Education (VOYCE).

14 UIC Institute for Policy and Civic Engagement (2022).

two categories: additional security personnel or social-emotional supports (e.g., social workers, interventionists, restorative justice coordinators).[15]

At the time of the Board resolution in 2020, CPS had experienced a years-long downward trend in reported disciplinary infractions, the use of exclusionary discipline (such as in-school and out-of-school suspension), and police notifications related to behavioral infractions. **Figure 2** shows the percentage of CPS high school students in each school year since 2014–15 with different disciplinary outcomes (solid lines). The proportion of students with discipline infractions, high-level infractions, suspensions, and police notifications declined each year through 2018–19. Data for 2019–20 and 2020–21 are not included due to pandemic-related disruptions to instruction and data collection. Between 2021–22 and 2022–23, there was an increase in each of these outcomes. Schools that fully removed SROs, either prior to or after the Board resolution, consistently had lower rates of discipline infractions, suspensions, and police notifications than schools that partially removed or retained both SROs.

While discipline outcomes trended down across the district, Student Physical Safety, Teacher Physical Safety, and Student-Teacher Trust all remained somewhat flat through 2018–19, with a peak in 2020–21 (except for Student Physical Safety which was not measured in that year) and then trended downward through 2022–23 (**Figure 3**).

FIGURE 2

Recorded discipline infractions, suspensions, and police notifications declined in CPS high schools from 2014–15 through 2018–19

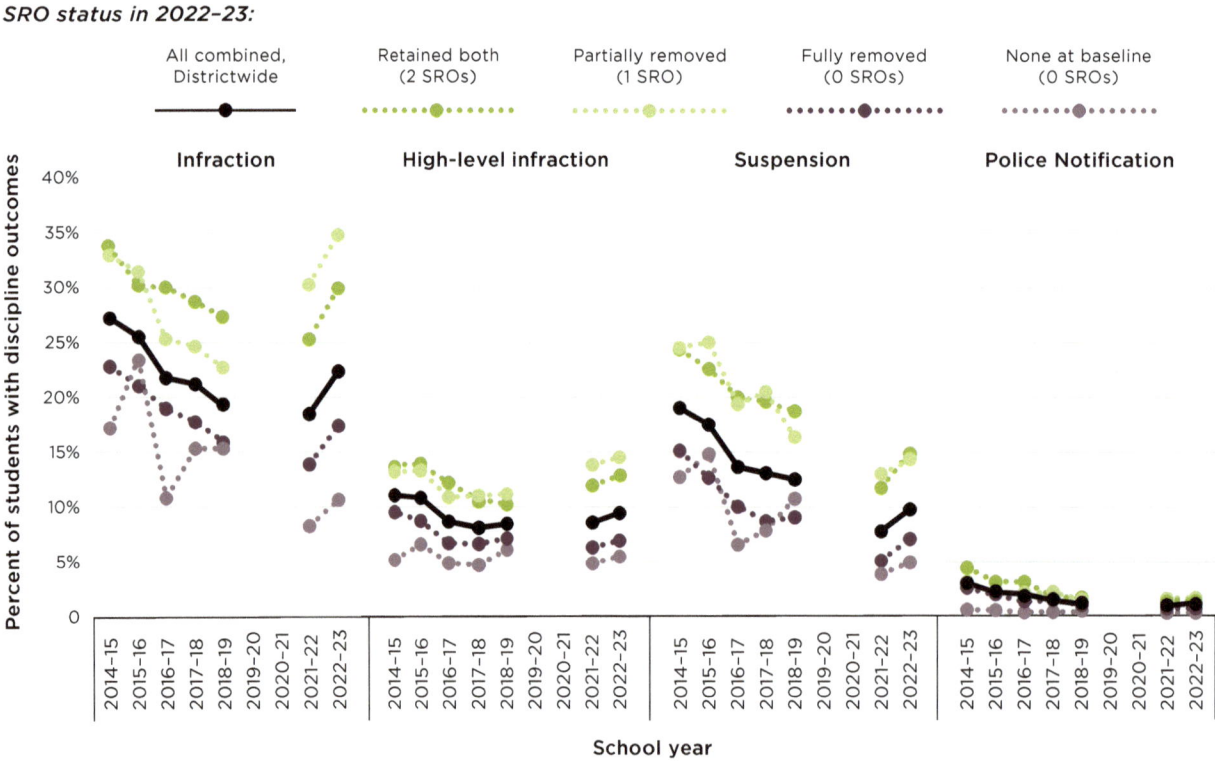

SRO status in 2022–23:

All combined, Districtwide — Retained both (2 SROs) — Partially removed (1 SRO) — Fully removed (0 SROs) — None at baseline (0 SROs)

Infraction — High-level infraction — Suspension — Police Notification

Note: Suspension includes both in-school and out-of-school suspension. Data for 2019–20 and 2020–21 are not reported due to disruptions in instruction and data collection related to the COVID-19 pandemic. See Table A.5 in Appendix A for the number of students included in each group and year. Figure A.2 in Appendix A provides graphs of the school-level trends over time for discipline outcomes.

15 A forthcoming research brief will provide details on the different ways schools spent reinvestment funds.

FIGURE 3

Student and Teacher Physical Safety and Student-Teacher Trust were flat through 2018–19 in CPS high schools, but trended downward starting in 2020–21

SRO status in 2022–23:

All combined, Districtwide	Retained both (2 SROs)	Partially removed (1 SRO)	Fully removed (0 SROs)	None at baseline (0 SROs)

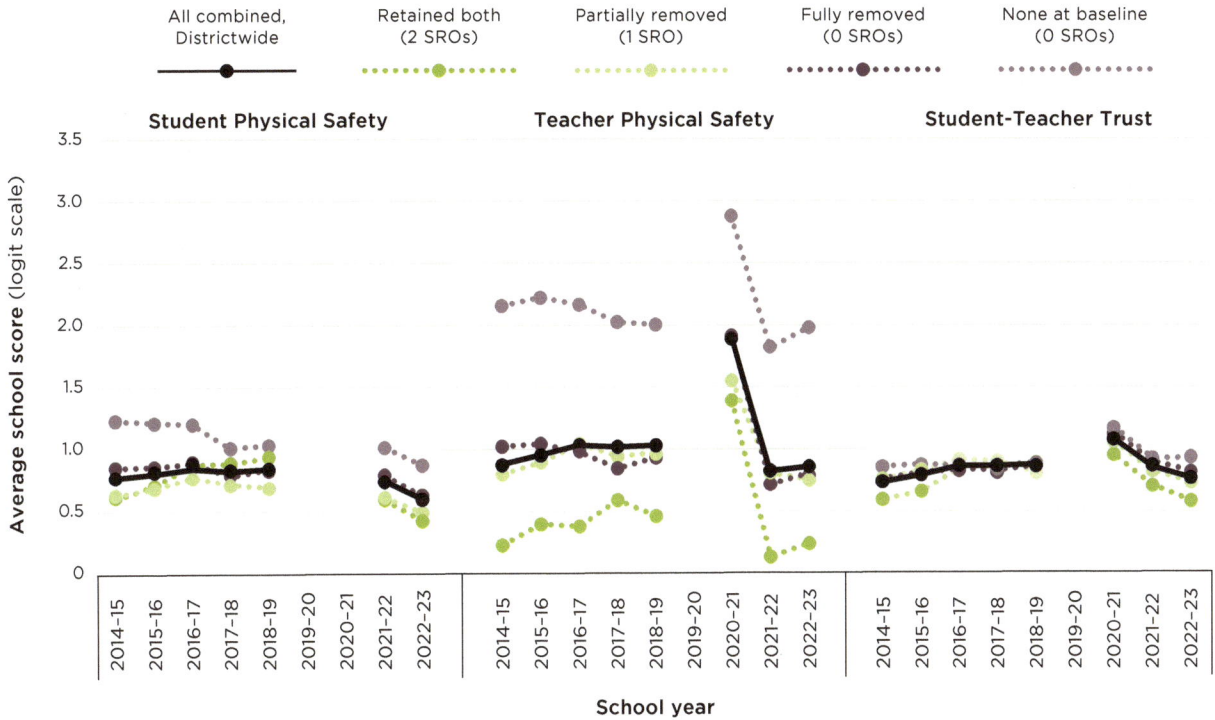

Note: The scores of different measures are on different scales and are not comparable to each other. Data for 2019–20 are not reported due to disruptions in instruction and data collection related to the COVID-19 pandemic. Only one Student Physical Safety item was administered in 2020–21 and measure scores were not calculated. See Table A.2 in Appendix A for the number of schools included in each group and year. Figure A.1 in Appendix A also provides graphs of the student-level trends in survey scores over time.

Findings

What were the characteristics of schools that retained, partially removed, or fully removed SROs?

- ### What were the characteristics of students in schools that made different decisions about SROs?

To understand the implications of the LSCs' choices for CPS students, we examined the demographics and characteristics of students who experienced different levels of SRO presence and removal.

Black students were most likely to be in schools that retained one or both SROs.

During the 2018–19 and 2019–20 school years, approximately 90% of CPS high school students had two SROs stationed inside their school. By 2022–23, that number declined to 21%, with an additional 17% having one SRO, and 62% of students in high schools with no SROs (see Figure B.1 in Appendix B).[16] Although the proportion of students with an SRO declined substantially for all race/ethnicity groups, large racialized differences emerged during implementation of the policy, as shown in **Figure 4**. In 2022–23, 63% of Black high school students had at least one SRO in their school, compared with 29% each for Latinx and White students, 22% for Asian/Pacific Islander students and 27% of students in additional race/ethnicity groups.

Students who were eligible for free or reduced-price lunch, students who were not English Learners, and students in special education were more likely to be in schools that retained one or both SROs than their peers.

We use free or reduced-price lunch eligibility as a proxy to identify students with socioeconomic disadvantage. A larger percentage of high school students eligible for free or reduced-price lunch (41%) attended a school that retained one or both SROs, compared with ineligible students (30%) in 2022–23 (**top panel of Figure 5 on p.10**).

Comparing high school students who were ever classified as an English Learner to those who never had that classification (**middle panel of Figure 5 on p.10**), a higher percentage of the "never English Learner" group attended a high school with at least one SRO (43% vs. 29%, respectively) in 2022–23.[17] Forty-two percent of students identified for Special Education services were in a school with an SRO presence in 2022–23, while 38% of students who did not receive Special Education services were (**bottom panel of Figure 5 on p.10**). There was no difference in SRO presence by student gender (results not shown).

---

16 There are differences between these percentages and the percent of schools with SROs because schools varied in enrollment, and small schools were less likely to remove SROs than large schools.

17 The "never English Learner" group was differentially comprised of Black students. Forty-five percent of the never English Learner group was Black, compared with 3% of current English Learners and 2% formerly classified as English Learners.

FIGURE 4

In 2022–23, most Black students had an SRO (1-2 SROs) in their high schools, while most Latinx, White, Asian/Pacific Islander/Hawaiian, and students in other race/ethnicity groups had no SRO presence in their school

SRO status in school year:

■ None at baseline (0 SROs)　■ Fully removed (0 SROs)　■ Partially removed (1 SRO)　■ Retained both (2 SROs)

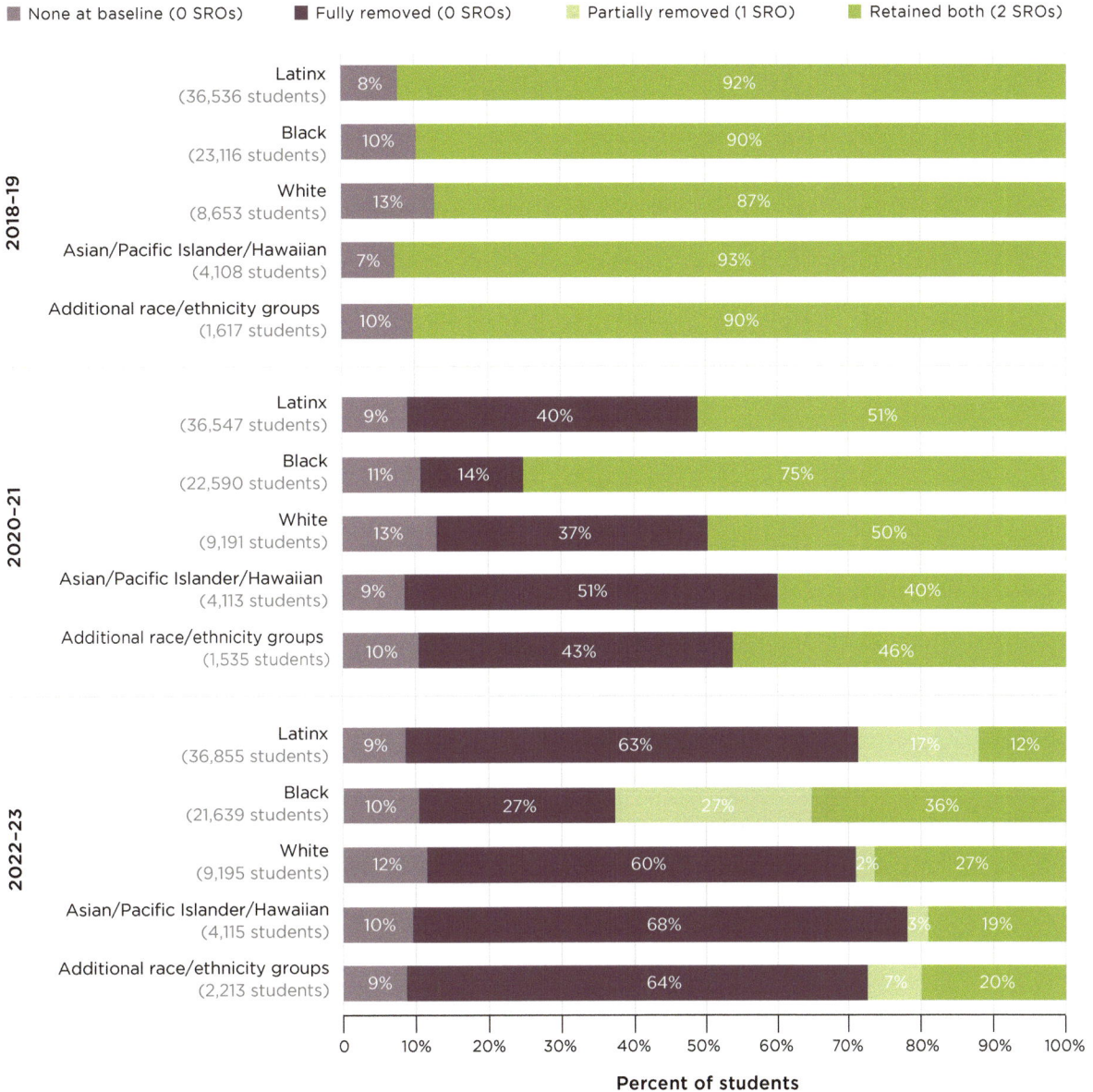

2018-19

Latinx (36,536 students)	8%		92%
Black (23,116 students)	10%		90%
White (8,653 students)	13%		87%
Asian/Pacific Islander/Hawaiian (4,108 students)	7%		93%
Additional race/ethnicity groups (1,617 students)	10%		90%

2020-21

Latinx (36,547 students)	9%	40%	51%
Black (22,590 students)	11%	14%	75%
White (9,191 students)	13%	37%	50%
Asian/Pacific Islander/Hawaiian (4,113 students)	9%	51%	40%
Additional race/ethnicity groups (1,535 students)	10%	43%	46%

2022-23

Latinx (36,855 students)	9%	63%	17%	12%
Black (21,639 students)	10%	27%	27%	36%
White (9,195 students)	12%	60%	2%	27%
Asian/Pacific Islander/Hawaiian (4,115 students)	10%	68%	3%	19%
Additional race/ethnicity groups (2,213 students)	9%	64%	7%	20%

Percent of students

Note: The additional race/ethnicity categories include Native American/Alaskan Native, Multiracial, and no reported race/ethnicity. These groups were combined due to small sample sizes rather than excluding these students from this reporting. Percentages within each category may not sum to 100% due to rounding.

Schools that retained one or both SROs tended to serve predominantly Black students.

To understand how high schools across CPS differed, we next examined what characteristics of schools were associated with choosing full or partial removal of SROs.

The racialized patterns at the student level reflect differences in the characteristics of high schools that removed SROs. Among the 17 high schools that retained both SROs through 2022–23, 11 served predominantly (80% or more) Black students and four served a student population 80% or more composed of both Black and Latinx students (**Figure 6 on p.10**). All schools serving predominantly Latinx students opted to remove at least one SRO.

FIGURE 5

Students' eligibility for free/reduced-price lunch, English Learner status, and special education status were associated with SRO presence in their high schools

SRO status in 2022–23:

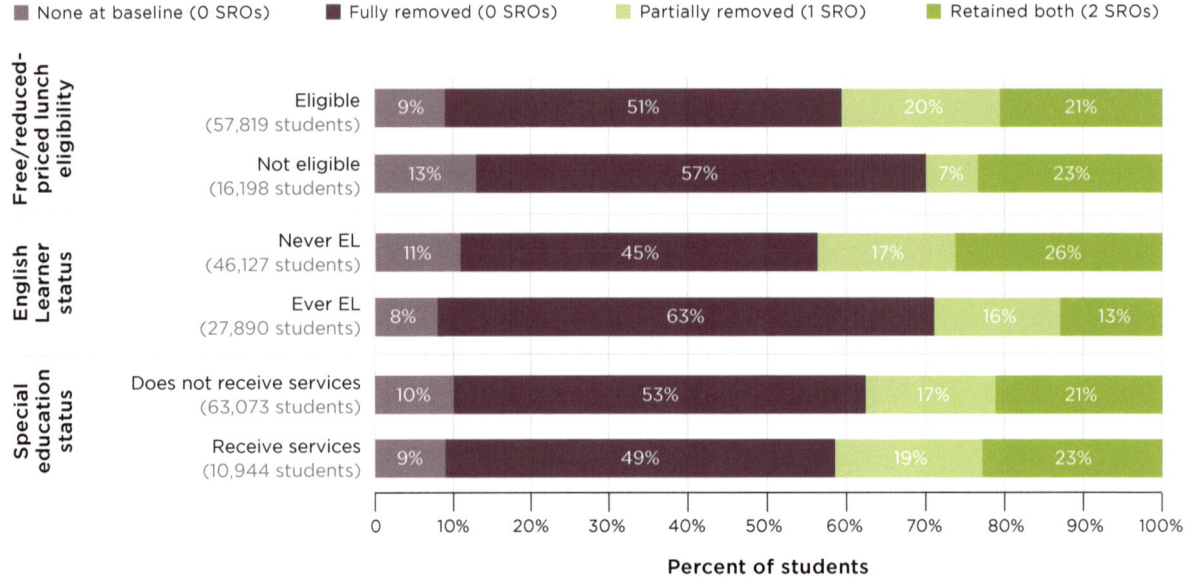

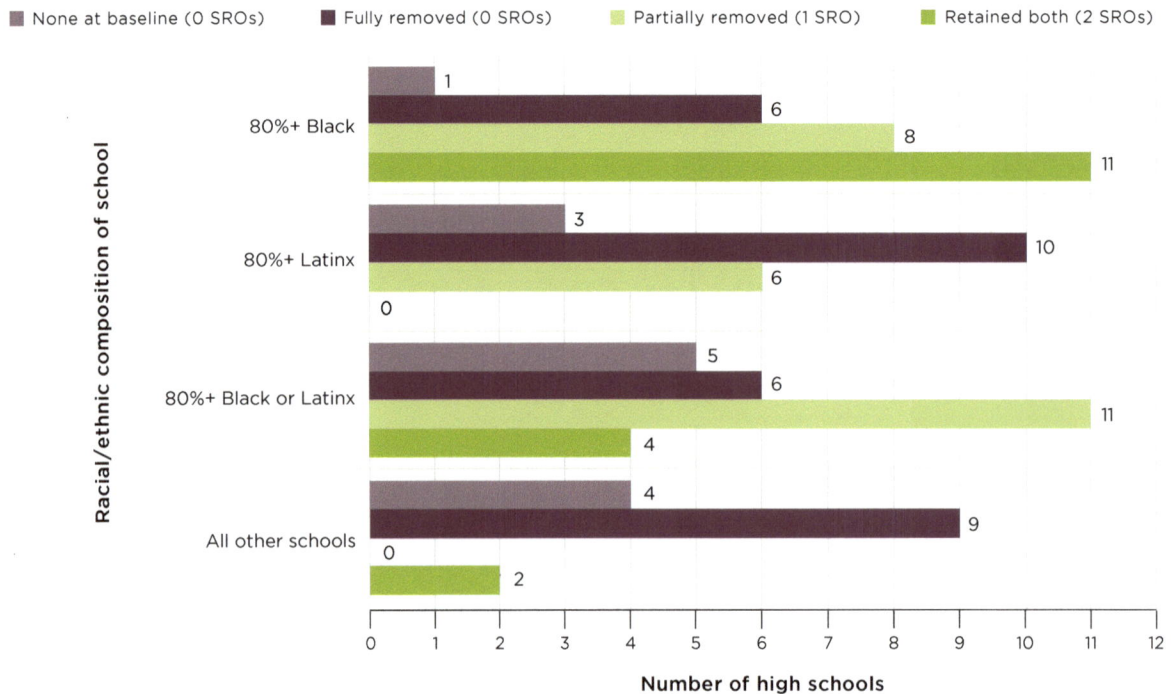

■ None at baseline (0 SROs)   ■ Fully removed (0 SROs)   ■ Partially removed (1 SRO)   ■ Retained both (2 SROs)

		None at baseline	Fully removed	Partially removed	Retained both
Free/reduced-priced lunch eligibility	Eligible (57,819 students)	9%	51%	20%	21%
	Not eligible (16,198 students)	13%	57%	7%	23%
English Learner status	Never EL (46,127 students)	11%	45%	17%	26%
	Ever EL (27,890 students)	8%	63%	16%	13%
Special education status	Does not receive services (63,073 students)	10%	53%	17%	21%
	Receive services (10,944 students)	9%	49%	19%	23%

Percent of students (0 to 100%)

Note: Percentages within each category may not sum to 100% due to rounding.

FIGURE 6

High schools that served predominantly Black students were the most likely to have retained both SROs through 2022–23

SRO status in 2022–23:

■ None at baseline (0 SROs)   ■ Fully removed (0 SROs)   ■ Partially removed (1 SRO)   ■ Retained both (2 SROs)

Racial/ethnic composition of school:

	None at baseline	Fully removed	Partially removed	Retained both
80%+ Black	1	6	8	11
80%+ Latinx	3	10	6	0
80%+ Black or Latinx	5	6	11	4
All other schools	4	9	0	2

Number of high schools (0 to 12)

Note: Schools were divided into mutually exclusive categories based on the racial/ethnic composition of their student population. Schools that served a population of more than 80% Black or Latinx students, but neither Black nor Latinx students made up 80% on their own were placed in the "80%+ Black or Latinx" group. Schools in the "All other schools" category had student populations that included more than 20% students in additional race/ethnicity groups.

High schools with more reported behavioral infractions and with higher suspension rates were more likely to have retained one or both SROs.

Measures of school discipline in 2022–23—the percent of students with a behavioral infraction, the percent of students with a high-level behavioral infraction, and the percent of students with a suspension—were related to having an SRO presence. The **top panel of Figure 7** shows the distribution of school choices when schools were split into three groups, based on the percent of students receiving a suspension during the school year. Specifically, of the 29 high schools with the lowest suspension rates in 2022–23, eight had an SRO presence (1-2 SROs). For the 29 high schools with the highest suspension rates, 22 had an SRO presence. There were similar patterns when we categorized schools by reported behavioral infractions and reported high-level behavioral infractions: the higher the infraction rate, the more likely that the school had retained both SROs (**Figure B.2 in Appendix B**).

Smaller schools and those serving economically disadvantaged students were more likely to have retained at least one SRO.

School enrollment and the proportion of economically disadvantaged students were also related to SRO presence (**Figure 7**). In 2022–23, 19 of the 29 high schools with the highest student enrollment had no SRO presence. In contrast, only seven of the smallest 29 high schools had no SRO presence while the other 22 had at least one SRO on campus (**middle panel of Figure 7**). Schools that served the lowest proportions of students with economic disadvantage (i.e., had the fewest students eligible for free or reduced-price lunch) were the most likely to have removed SROs prior to the 2020 Board resolution; 10 of the 13 schools that had no SROs at baseline were in this group (**bottom panel of Figure 7**).

Among the 29 high schools serving less than 84% students eligible for free or reduced-price lunch, 22 had no SROs. Of the 29 high schools serving the highest proportion of free or reduced-price lunch eligible students (92% or higher), only nine had no SROs.

FIGURE 7

High schools that retained SROs had higher suspension rates, were smaller, and served fewer socioeconomically disadvantaged students

SRO status in 2022–23:

■ None at baseline (0 SROs) ■ Fully removed (0 SROs) ■ Partially removed (1 SRO) ■ Retained both (2 SROs)

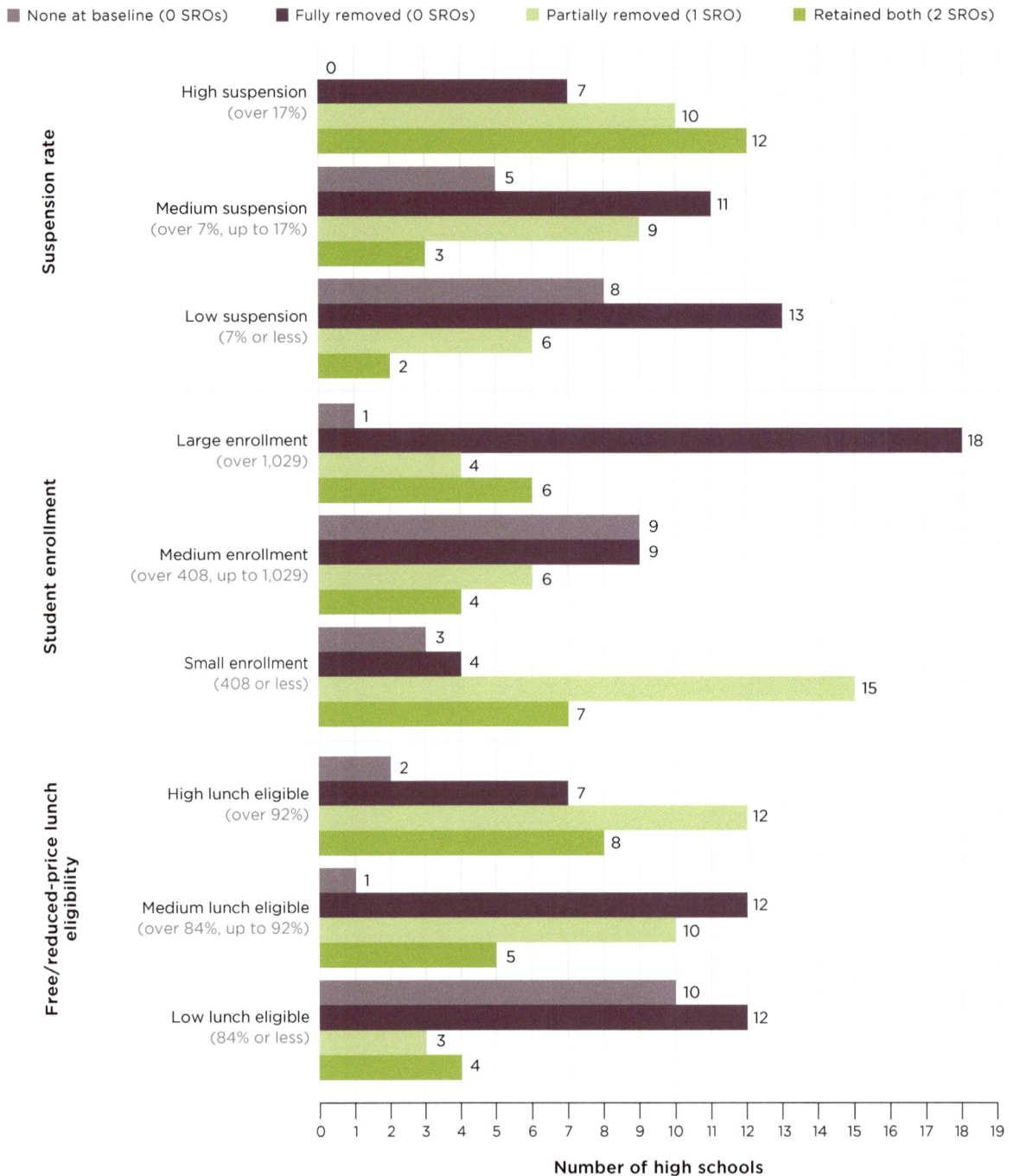

Suspension rate

High suspension (over 17%)
- None at baseline: 0
- Fully removed: 7
- Partially removed: 10
- Retained both: 12

Medium suspension (over 7%, up to 17%)
- None at baseline: 5
- Fully removed: 11
- Partially removed: 9
- Retained both: 3

Low suspension (7% or less)
- None at baseline: 8
- Fully removed: 13
- Partially removed: 6
- Retained both: 2

Student enrollment

Large enrollment (over 1,029)
- None at baseline: 1
- Fully removed: 18
- Partially removed: 4
- Retained both: 6

Medium enrollment (over 408, up to 1,029)
- None at baseline: 9
- Fully removed: 9
- Partially removed: 6
- Retained both: 4

Small enrollment (408 or less)
- None at baseline: 3
- Fully removed: 4
- Partially removed: 15
- Retained both: 7

Free/reduced-price lunch eligibility

High lunch eligible (over 92%)
- None at baseline: 2
- Fully removed: 7
- Partially removed: 12
- Retained both: 8

Medium lunch eligible (over 84%, up to 92%)
- None at baseline: 1
- Fully removed: 12
- Partially removed: 10
- Retained both: 5

Low lunch eligible (84% or less)
- None at baseline: 10
- Fully removed: 12
- Partially removed: 3
- Retained both: 4

Number of high schools

Note: Categories for each school characteristic were created by dividing schools into three equal-sized groups, based on the school-level percent of students with a suspension, enrollment, and percent of students eligible for free/reduced-price lunch. Analysis of schools by the percent of students with an infraction and by the percent of students with a high-level infraction was qualitatively, similar to the analysis shown for suspension (see Appendix B).

When CPS high schools removed one or both SROs, how did school climate and discipline outcomes change?

Methods

To quantify how student- and school-level discipline and climate outcomes changed with the removal of SROs, we employed a difference-in-difference analysis. We chose this approach because the decisions to remove or retain SROs were not random: many school-level characteristics, policies, and contexts could have influenced both the SRO decision and the outcomes of interest. As shown in **Figure 2 on p.6**, schools that fully removed SROs by 2022–23 tended to have fewer discipline infractions and police notifications, even going back as far as 2014–15 when SROs were present in those schools. There were pre-existing differences in outcomes among schools who retained, partially removed, or fully removed SROs from their schools.

The difference-in-difference approach allows us to separate changes arising from SRO removal from other explanatory factors including, importantly, trends over time. To do this, we compared outcomes in 2018–19 between schools that later partially removed or fully removed SROs and schools that retained both (called the first difference).[18] Then, we compared outcomes after the policy change (in 2022–23) for the same groups (called the second difference). In these comparisons, we controlled for observed student and school characteristics, so that we were comparing schools and students that were as similar as possible—and not comparing outcomes of schools with very different contexts. If the first and second differences were different, then that is evidence consistent with the notion that SRO removal explains changes in outcomes.[19] Another limitation to keep in mind with these results is that schools are relatively early in their implementation of SRO removal. Because an important element of the WSS Framework is shifting school climate, which may include but extends far beyond the act of removing SROs, it may take multiple consecutive years of implementation of alternate strategies to see significant effects.

SRO removal was not significantly related to the changes in discipline infractions.

While discipline infractions increased districtwide in 2022–23 compared to 2018–19, our analyses did not detect a relationship between these changes at the student (**Table C.1 in Appendix C**) nor school (**Table C.2**) levels and the removal of SROs.

SRO removal was significantly related to the changes in high-level discipline infractions.

In schools that fully removed SROs, students' probabilities of having a high-level behavioral infraction increased less than for students in schools that retained SROs.

High-level infractions were higher districtwide in 2022–23 compared to 2018–19 (**see Figure 2 on p.6**), but the trend was significantly different for students in schools that had fully removed SROs compared to those that retained both. This is illustrated in **Figure 8.** The dark green line (retained both SROs) shows that the chances of a high-level infraction were higher in 2022–23 than in 2018–19 for students in schools that retained both SROs. The dotted lines represent what we would have expected for students in schools that partially and fully removed SROs, *if there was no effect of SRO removal*. However, we see that the actual rate in 2022–23 for students in schools that fully removed SROs is lower than that expectation by 2.2 percentage points. This is the difference-in-difference estimate, and it is statistically significant. The 1.3 percentage point difference for students in schools that partially removed SROs was not statistically significant. Further, while the chance of a high-level infraction, on average, increased over the time

---

18 We excluded high schools that did not have SROs prior to the baseline year of 2018-19 from the difference-in-difference analysis.

19 This approach can have a causal interpretation (i.e., the estimates capture the impact of SRO removal) if a set of important assumptions are met; we provide a discussion and more detail in Appendix C. We do not think all assumptions are met to say that SRO removal was the sole reason for observed differences, but reporting these differences, which have been adjusted for many observed school and student-level characteristics, does provide a "like-with-like" interpretation of results.

period for students in schools that retained one or both SROs (those solid lines have positive slopes), it remained steady for students in schools that fully removed SROs (purple line is nearly flat).

At the school level, the typical number of high-level disciplinary infractions in schools that retained both SROs was 118 in 2018–19 and 173 in 2022–23, an increase of 55 high-level infractions (**Figure 9**). In schools that fully removed SROs (purple lines), the typical increase over time was just 13 (from 116 in 2018–19 to 129 in 2022–23) which is 42 high-level infractions lower than the expectation *if there was no effect of SRO removal* and is statistically significant. For schools that partially removed SROs (light green lines), the difference-in-difference

FIGURE 8

Student probability of a high-level behavioral infraction was lower than predicted in high schools that removed SROs

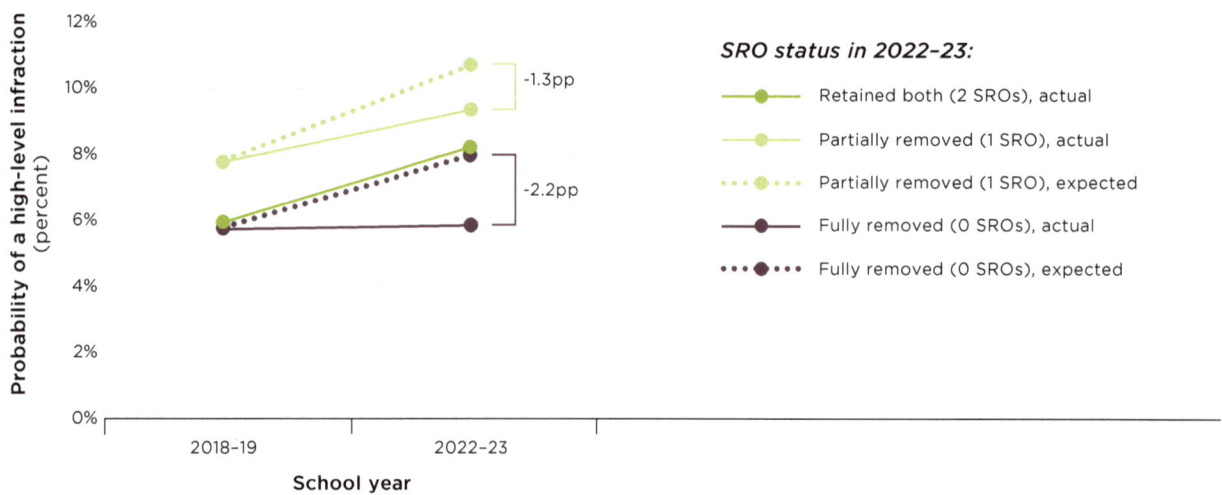

Note: See Table C.3 in Appendix C for difference-in-difference model estimates. The dotted lines (the expectation of the trend in the Partially and Fully removed groups) may not appear parallel with the darkest solid line (Retained both, control group) due to the nonlinear transformation in the logistic regression model that produced these results.

FIGURE 9

The number of high-level behavioral infractions was lower than expected in high schools that removed both SROs

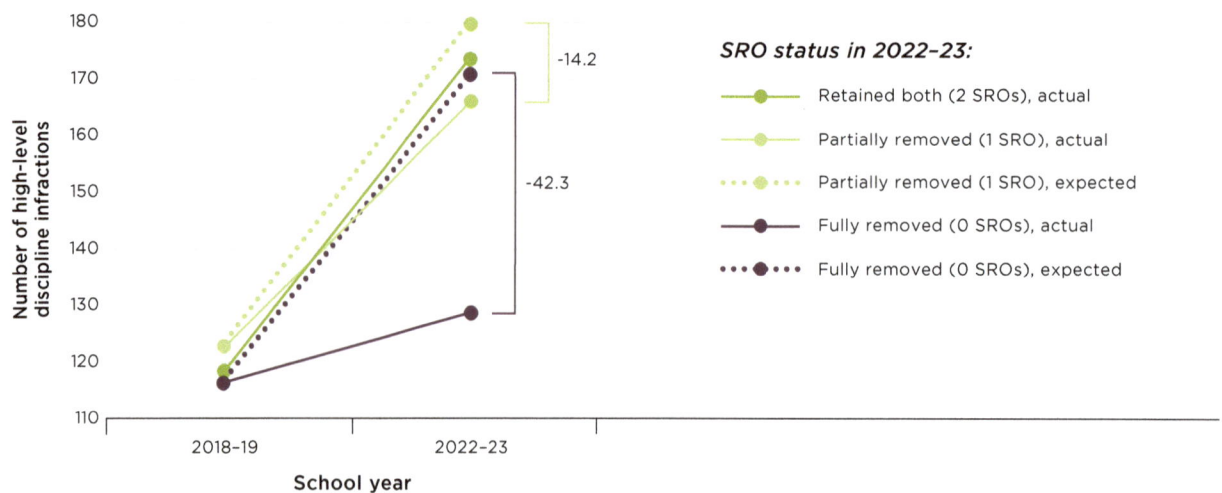

Note: See Table C.3 in Appendix C for difference-in-difference model estimates. The dotted lines (the expectation of the trend in the Partially and Fully removed groups) may not appear parallel with the darkest solid line (Retained both, control group) due to the nonlinear transformation of counts in the Poisson regression model that produced these results.

approach suggests that there were approximately 14 fewer high-level behavioral infractions than predicted.

SRO removal was not significantly related to the changes in suspensions.

We examined suspensions, inclusive of in-school and out-of-school, at both the school and student levels. The trends for the partial and full removal categories were not significantly different than for schools that retained both SROs (**Tables C5 and C6**).

SRO removal was not significantly related to the changes in police notifications.

High schools that fully removed SROs had a steeper drop in the number of police notifications in 2022–23 than did schools that retained both SROs. This difference-in-difference was not statistically significant, but it was substantively large. Statistical significance depends on having a large enough sample to be certain the results did not occur by random chance. In the case of the school analyses, there were small numbers of schools in each of the SRO categories, making it difficult to find differences to be statistically significant, even if they were large. Because we base our analyses on the population of schools in the district, we can say with certainty that these were the differences observed in police notifications by SRO groups, we just cannot be certain they did not occur by

random chance. **Figure 10** shows the differences in the predictions of the number of police notifications for the different SRO presence categories.

SRO removal was not significantly related to changes in student perceptions of physical safety.

From 2018–19 to 2022–23, there was a districtwide decrease in student perception of physical safety across high schools (see Figure 3) and this trend held in the different SRO presence categories of schools and for their students (**see Tables C.9 and C.10 in Appendix C**).

SRO removal was not significantly related to changes in teacher perceptions of physical safety.

From 2018–19 to 2022–23, there was a slight decrease in teacher perception of physical safety districtwide (**see Figure 3 on p.7**). We did not detect a significant difference-in-difference for schools that partially or fully removed SROs as compared to schools that retained both (**see Table C.11 in Appendix C**).

SRO removal was not significantly related to changes in Student-Teacher Trust.

We did not detect significant differences in the Student-Teacher Trust trends with partial or full removal of SROs at the student or school levels (**see Tables C.12 and C.13 in Appendix C**).

FIGURE 10

Police notifications declined with the full removal of SROs, but the difference was not statistically significant

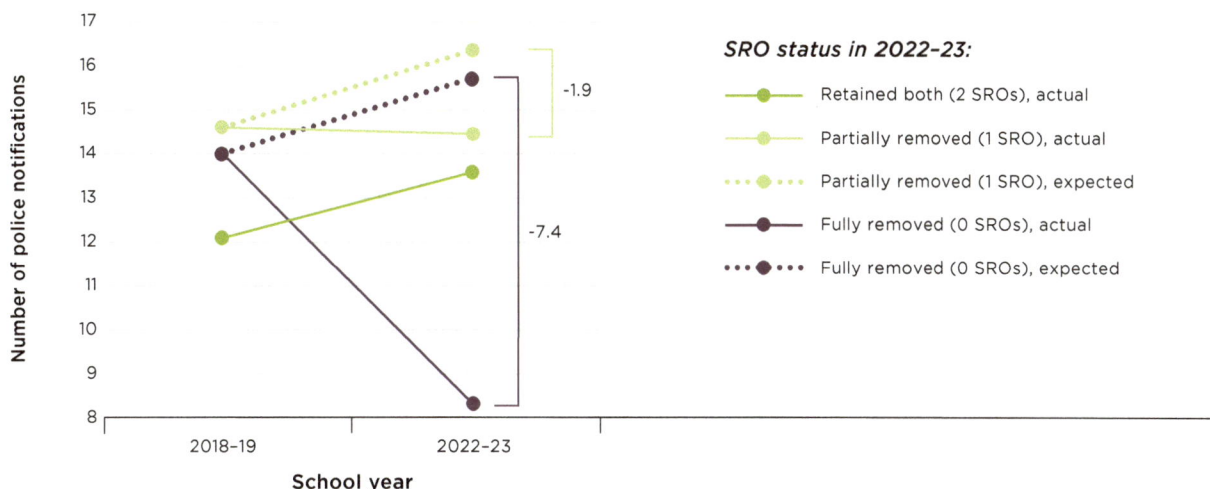

Note: See Table C.3 in Appendix C for difference-in-difference model estimates. The dotted lines (the expectation of the trend in the Partially and Fully removed groups) may not appear parallel with the darkest solid line (Retained both, control group) due to the nonlinear transformation of counts in the Poisson regression model that produced these results.

Interpretive summary

In Chicago, the relevance of this analysis for policy is clear: the Chicago Board of Education voted to remove SROs from all CPS schools starting in 2024–25. The analysis we conducted can inform this conversation, but we also recognize that questions about the presence of police in schools are complex and reflect differences in lived experiences and perspectives across policymakers, practitioners, young people, families, and communities.

In this study, we found:

The individual decisions of LSCs collectively led to differences in the presence of SROs by student race.

When individual LSCs determined whether to retain SROs, their collective individual decisions had district-wide equity implications. Although students in all groups we examined were much less likely to have an SRO in their school in 2022–23 compared to 2018–19, differences by student population emerged alongside the shift away from SROs. In particular, Black students became more than twice as likely as other students to have an SRO in their school.

Schools removed SROs without detrimental changes in student disciplinary outcomes or perceptions of school climate.

There were few significant changes associated with SRO removal, and the changes that occurred tended to be improvements. One outcome—the number of high-level infractions—showed a statistically significant decline when SROs were fully removed. And the numbers of police notifications were cut approximately in half, on average, in schools which fully removed SROs, although the difference was not statistically significant. Data on discipline infractions and police notifications can be unreliable as an indicator of safety in a school because it relies on whether incidents are reported or not. For that

reason, student and teacher reports can provide information on whether there has been a change in safety. The absence of evidence to suggest that removing police from schools led to changes in how safe students and teachers felt is important information, although individual experiences and perspectives on this point may vary and more years of data may be needed to establish this as a trend.

The methods and analyses used provide a compelling "like-with-like" interpretation of results because we accounted for differences in observed school and student-level characteristics. But this analysis alone does not establish causation; changes, or lack of changes, in discipline and school climate outcomes could arise from factors other than SRO removal. Nor does this analysis examine the underlying mechanisms that led to our findings.

For example, the removal of SROs in some schools was accompanied by compensatory funding for other safety-related supports like school-based security personnel, social workers, interventionists, and restorative justice coordinators. The availability of those additional adults may have helped improve students' and teachers' experiences and school culture overall. Our findings are likely best interpreted as due to the combination of SRO removal with alternate spending. As CPS continues to implement SRO removal and expand the WSS Framework districtwide, there is need for continued attention to how these policies shift student experiences overall, and for different groups of students.

We will provide additional insights in ongoing research—including whether SRO removal changed outcomes for particular groups of students, how schools chose to reinvest the funds made available by SRO removal, and how districtwide practices and outcomes continue to evolve over time and with the districtwide expansion of the WSS Framework.

References

Chrusciel, M.M., Wolfe, S., Hansen, J.A., Rojek, J.J., & Kaminski, R. (2015)
Law enforcement executive and principal perspectives on school safety measures: School Resource Officers and armed school employees. *Policing: An International Journal of Police Strategies and Management, 38*(1), 24-39.

Cobbina, J.E., Galasso, M., Cunningham, M., Melde, C., & Heinze, J. (2020)
A qualitative study of perception of school safety among youth in a high crime city. *Journal of School Violence, 19*(3), 277-291.

Curran, F.C., & Boza, L. (2023)
Community policing in schools and School Resource Officer transparency. *Educational Policy, 37*(6), 1573-1602.

Curran, F.C., Viano, S., Kupchik, A., & Fisher, B.W. (2021)
Do interactions with School Resource Officers predict students' likelihood of being disciplined and feelings of safety? Mixed-methods evidence from two school districts. *Educational Evaluation and Policy Analysis, 43*(2), 200-232.

Fisher, B.W., & Hennessy, E.A. (2016)
School Resource Officers and exclusionary discipline in U.S. high schools: A systematic review and meta-analysis. *Adolescent Research Review, 1*(3), 217-233.

Gottfredson, D.C., Crosse, S., Tang, Z., Bauer, E.L., Harmon, M.A., Hagen, C.A., & Greene, A.D. (2020)
Effects of school resource officers on school crime and responses to school crime. *Criminology & Public Policy, 19*(3), 905-940.

Hart, H., Young, C., Chen, A., Zou, A., & Allensworth, E.M. (2020)
Supporting school improvement: Early findings from reexamination of the 5Essentials *survey*. Chicago, IL: University of Chicago Consortium on School Research.

Javdani, S. (2019)
Policing education: An empirical review of the challenges and impact of the work of school police officers. *American Journal of Community Psychology, 63*(3-4), 253-269.

Kurtz, H. (2020, June 26)
Educators support Black Lives Matter, but still want police in schools, survey shows. *Education Week*. Retrieved from https://www.edweek.org/leadership/educators-support-black-lives-matter-but-still-want-police-in-schools-survey-shows/2020/06

Layton, D., & Gerstenblatt, P. (2022)
"They're just, like, there": A constructivist grounded theory study of student experiences with school resource officers. *Journal of Community Psychology, 50*(8), 3470-3486.

Owens, E.G. (2017)
Testing the school-to-prison pipeline. *Journal of Policy Analysis and Management, 36*(1), 11-37.

Riser-Kositsky, M., Sawchuk, S., & Peele, H. (2021, June 4).
School police: Which districts cut them? Which brought them back? *Education Week*. Retrieved from https://www.edweek.org/leadership/which-districts-have-cut-school-policing-programs/2021/06

Sorensen, L.C., Avila-Acosta, M., Engberg, J.B., & Bushway, S.D. (2023)
The thin blue line in schools: New evidence on school-based policing across the U.S. *Journal of Policy Analysis and Management, 42*(4), 941-970.

Theriot, M.T. (2016)
The impact of School Resource Officer interaction on students' feelings about school and school police. *Crime & Delinquency, 62*(4), 446–469.

Theriot, M.T., & Orme, J.G. (2016)
School Resource Officers and students' feelings of safety at school. *Youth Violence and Juvenile Justice, 14*(2), 130-146.

UIC Institute for Policy and Civic Engagement. (2022)
Whole School Safety Plan recommendations process: Documentation, observations, and recommendations. Chicago, IL: University of Illinois-Chicago.

Wang, K., Kemp, J., & Burr, R. (2022)
Crime, violence, discipline, and safety in U.S. public schools: Findings from the School Survey on Crime and Safety: 2019-20 (NCES 2022-029). Washington, DC: National Center for Education Statistics.

Weisburst, E.K. (2019)
Patrolling public schools: The impact of funding for school police on student discipline and long-term education outcomes. *Journal of Policy Analysis and Management, 38*(2), 338-365.

Wolfe, S.E., Chrusciel, M.M., Rojek, J., Hansen, J.A., & Kaminski, R.J. (2017)
Procedural justice, legitimacy, and school principals' evaluations of School Resource Officers: Support, perceived effectiveness, trust, and satisfaction. *Criminal Justice Policy Review, 28*(2), 107-138.

Zhang, G. (2019)
The effects of a school policing program on crime, discipline, and disorder: A quasi-experimental evaluation. *American Journal of Criminal Justice, 44*(1), 45-62.

Appendix A
Sample and variables

Analytic samples

All analyses in this brief include district-run high schools in Chicago Public Schools (CPS) that were operational in a given school year. Charter schools are not included as they were not subject to the same policies related to school resource officers (SROs). Additionally, we excluded other schools that were not subject to the "status quo" of having two SROs prior to the 2020 Board of Education resolution that established the process for removal of SROs: Options (alternative), virtual, and special education schools. Student-level analyses include all students enrolled in grades 9-12 in the included schools in the given school year. The total number of high schools and 9-12 students per year is provided in **Table A.1**.

TABLE A.1

Number of operational district-run high schools and students in grades 9–12 enrolled by year

School year	High schools	9-12 students
2014–15	91	80,725
2015–16	90	78,278
2016–17	89	76,036
2017–18	89	75,310
2018–19	87	74,030
2019–20	87	73,912
2020–21	87	73,976
2021–22	86	73,880
2022–23	86	74,017

For the difference-in-difference analyses of discipline and climate outcomes, we further restricted the school-level sample to the 72 high schools meeting the above criteria that were open continuously from our baseline year of 2018–19 through 2022–23 and that had two SROs in the baseline year. Additionally, we excluded one high school that was missing *5Essentials* Survey and other annual survey data in 2017–18, 2018–19, or 2022–23. **This yields a sample of 142 school by year observations: 71 in 2018–19 and 71 in 2022–23**

The student-level sample for the impact analysis included all students enrolled in grades 9-12 the 72 district-run schools that were open continuously from 2018–19 through 2022–23 and that had two SROs in the baseline year. Because we use school fixed-effects in the student-level difference-in-difference models, we did not have to exclude students in the school that was missing *5Essentials* Survey data. We did, however, have to exclude 5,422 observations of students in four schools that had no variation in our outcomes, as the model is not estimable. Six more observations were dropped due to missing data (no race/ethnicity). **This yielded a sample of 98,124 student-by-year observations: 49,682 in 2018–19 and 48,442 in 2022–23**. There are 97,749 unique students in our sample (some students had observations in both years) across 68 schools.

For the survey outcomes, we had to further reduce our sample to students with scores. Students may not have responded to the survey or their scores may not have been estimable or dropped for other technical reasons (e.g., too few items, misfit). We kept students who had both a Student Physical Safety and Teacher-Student Trust score. **This leads to a sample of 66,043 student-by-year observations: 37,025 in 2018–19 and 29,018 in 2022–23**. There are 66,019 unique students in our sample (some students had observations in both years) across 68 schools.

Outcome variables

The *5Essentials* Survey results and supplementary measure scores were estimated using Rasch family models. Note that different measure scales are not comparable. For example, we cannot make direct comparisons between the Student Physical Safety scores to the Teacher Physical Safety scores to claim that students felt less safe than teachers.

For the school-level analyses, we used the *5Essentials* Survey school scores calibrated from the Rasch model. These scores were on the logit scale and were precision-weighted using an individual-level weight of the inverse of the standard error. For the student-level scores, we used the logit scale.

The *Student Physical Safety* measure is the School Safety measure from the *5Essentials* Survey. We renamed it for the purpose of this brief, to differentiate it from the teacher measure and to make it clear that it covers only the physical safety pillar of the Whole School Safety (WSS) Framework adopted by CPS.

The measure contains five items with the stem "How safe do you feel...?" which students rated on a scale of: **1)** Not safe; **2)** Somewhat safe; **3)** Mostly safe; **4)** Very safe.

- In the hallways of the school
- In the bathrooms of the school
- Outside around the school
- Traveling between home and school
- In your classes

Both student-level and school-level scores were calculated from these items. The average school scores over time are shown in **Figure 3 on p.7** in the main text. The number of schools that contributed to each average are provided in **Table A.2**. The average student scores over time are shown in **Figure A.1** and the number of students in each average in **Table A.3**.

The *Teacher Physical Safety* measure is a supplementary measure on the CPS annual survey. It is not directly aligned to the *5Essentials* Survey framework. There are seven items with the stem "To what extent is each of the following a problem at your school?"

which teachers rate on a scale of: **1)** Not at all; **2)** A little; **3)** Some; **4)** To a great extent.

- Physical conflicts among students
- Robbery or theft
- Gang activity
- Disorder in classrooms
- Disorder in hallways
- Student disrespect of teachers
- Threats of violence towards teachers

The Teacher Physical Safety items are reverse coded which means that the "higher" responses actually indicate a lower perception of physical safety. As such, the scores reported in this brief are transformed to their opposite (multiplied by -1) for interpretability. The average school scores over time are shown in **Figure 3 on p.7** in the main text. The number of schools that contributed to each average are provided in **Table A.2**.

The *Student-Teacher Trust* measure is a student measure from the *5Essentials* Survey. The measure contains five items with the stem "How much do you disagree or agree with the following statements?" which students rate on a scale of: **1)** Strongly disagree; **2)** Disagree; **3)** Agree; **4)** Strongly agree.

- I feel safe with my teachers at this school
- I feel comfortable with my teachers at this school
- My teachers always keep their promises
- My teachers always listen to students' ideas
- My teachers treat me with respect

TABLE A.2

Number of students in each group and year (each "dot" in Figure 3)

SRO status in 2022-23	2014-15	2015-16	2016-17	2017-18	2018-19	2019-20	2020-21	2021-22	2022-23
All combined, districtwide	91	89-90	89	88-89	86	0	86	78-80	86
Retained both (2 SROs)	17	17	17	17	17	0	17	15-16	17
Partially removed (1 SRO)	23	23	24	24	24	0	24	24	25
Fully removed (0 SROs)	31	31	31	31	31	0	31	28	31
None at baseline (0 SROs)	13	13	13	13	13	0	13	10-13	13

Note: Ranges are provided where the number of schools contributing to the average differed among the measures. This happened because some schools were missing one or more survey measures in any given year.

Both student-level and school-level scores are calculated from these items. The average school scores over time are shown in **Figure 3 on p.7** in the main text. The number of schools that contributed to each average are provided in **Table A.2**. The average student scores over time are shown in **Figure A.1** and the number of students in each average in **Table A.3**.

We examined high-level **discipline infractions**, the annual count of high-level infractions at the school-level and whether a student had a high-level discipline

FIGURE A.1

Average student survey scores over time

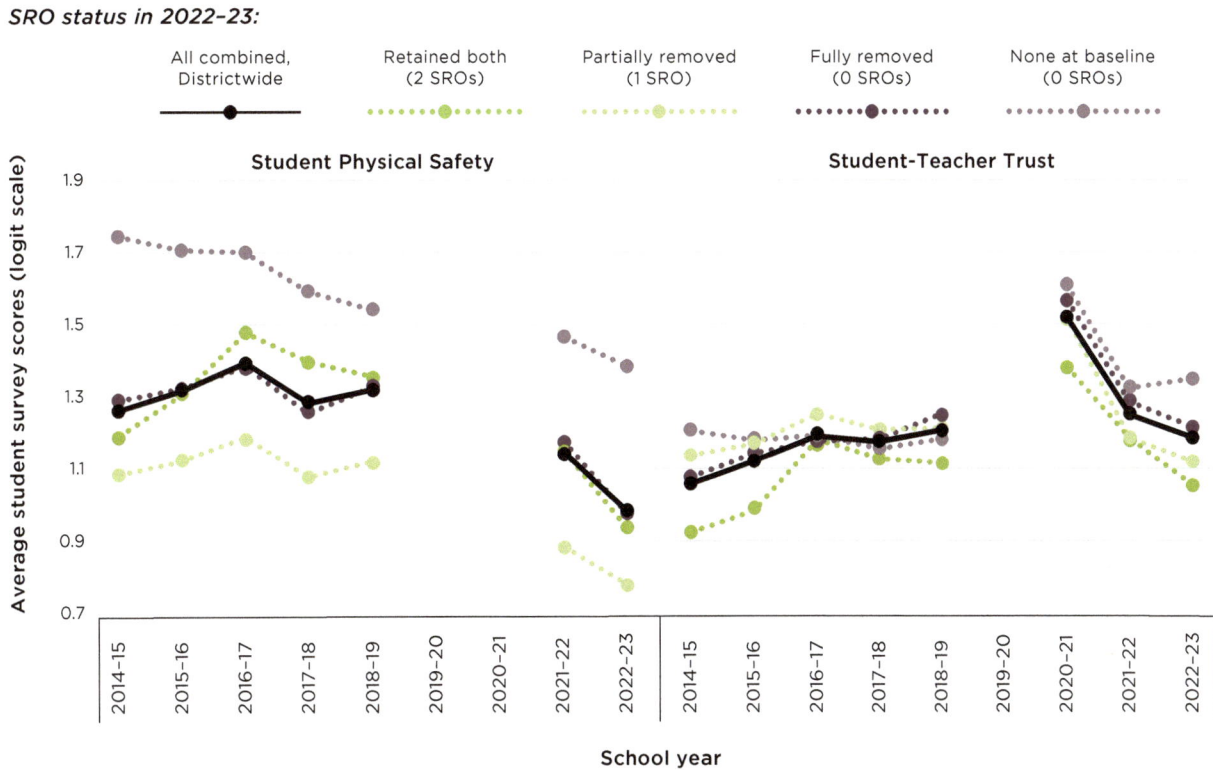

SRO status in 2022–23:

Note: The scores of different measures are on different scales and are not comparable to each other. Data for 2019–20 are not reported due to disruptions in instruction and data collection related to the COVID-19 pandemic. Only one Student Physical Safety item was administered in 2020–21 and measure scores were not calculated.

TABLE A.3

Number of students in each student survey average shown in Figure A.1

SRO status in 2022-23	2014-15	2015-16	2016-17	2017-18	2018-19	2019-20	2020-21	2021-22	2022-23
All combined, districtwide	57,970–58,593	59,691–60,336	57,528–58,265	47,400–55,711	54,880–56,068	0	34,010	41,756–43,148	44,674–45,551
Retained both (2 SROs)	12,757–12,920	12,070–12,223	11,432–11,616	8,849–10,417	10,441–10,678	0	8,353	7,480 –7,751	7,756–7,930
Partially removed (1 SRO)	10,127–10,220	9,943–10,038	9,835–9,961	7,718–9,089	8,867–9,036	0	5,632	7,870–8,139	7,060–7,199
Fully removed (0 SROs)	28,712–29,010	31,434–31,762	30,354–30,719	26,042–30,617	29,901–30,565	0	15,446	22,622–23,354	24,661–25,152
None at baseline (0 SROs)	5,303–5,347	5,464–5,522	5,477–5,536	4,536–5,299	5,585–5,703	0	4,562	3,784–3,904	5,197–5,270

Note: Ranges are provided where the number of respondents differed among the measures.

infraction within a school year. Trends over time in school-level counts of high-level infractions are shown in **Figure A.2** with relevant Ns in **Table A.4**. Trends in the percentage of students who had a high-level discipline infraction are shown in **Figure 2 on p.6** in the main text, and the number of students in the denominator of each percentage is provided in **Table A.5**.

We examined **suspensions**, the annual count of suspensions at the school-level and whether a student had a suspension within a school year. Both in-school and out-of-school suspensions are included as we intend to summarize trends and differences in exclusionary discipline. Trends over time in school-level counts of suspensions are shown in **Figure A.2** with relevant Ns

in **Table A.4**. Trends in the percentage of students who had a suspension are shown in **Figure A.2** in the main text, and the number of students in the denominator of each percentage is provided in **Table A.5**.

We examined **police notifications**, the annual count of police notifications related to discipline infractions at the school-level and the whether a student had a police notification within a school year. Trends over time in school-level counts of police notifications are shown in **Figure A.2** with relevant Ns in **Table A.4**. Trends in the percentage of students who had a police notification are shown in **Figure 2 on p.6** in the main text, and the number of students in the denominator of each percentage is provided in **Table A.5**.

FIGURE A.2

Average number of discipline outcomes across schools over time

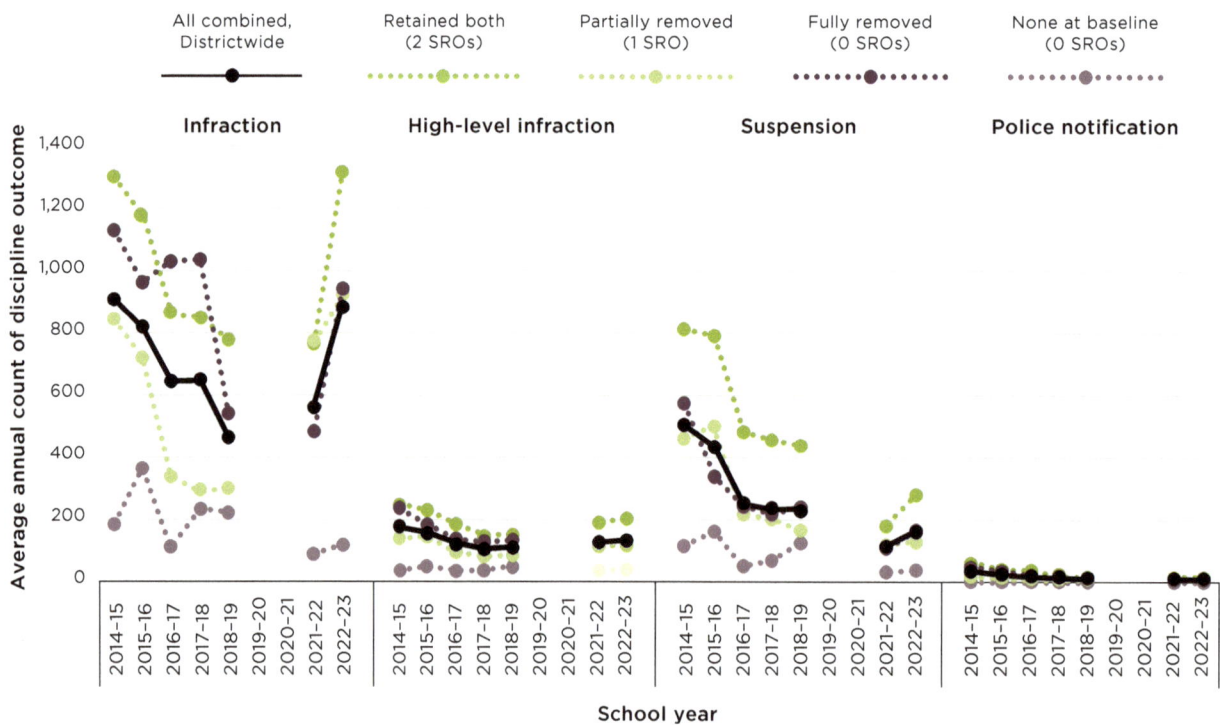

SRO status in 2022–23;

Note: Suspension includes both in-school and out-of-school suspension. Data for 2019–20 and 2020–21 are not reported due to disruptions in instruction and data collection related to the COVID-19 pandemic.

TABLE A.4

Number of schools in each group and year (each "dot" in Figure A.2)

SRO status in 2022-23	2014-15	2015-16	2016-17	2017-18	2018-19	2019-20	2020-21	2021-22	2022-23
All combined, districtwide	91	90	89	89	87	0	0	86	86
Retained both (2 SROs)	17	17	17	17	17	0	0	17	17
Partially removed (1 SRO)	23	23	24	24	24	0	0	25	25
Fully removed (0 SROs)	31	31	31	31	31	0	0	31	31
None at baseline (0 SROs)	13	13	13	13	13	0	0	13	13

TABLE A.5

Number of students in each proportion shown in Figure 2

SRO status in 2022-23	2014-15	2015-16	2016-17	2017-18	2018-19	2019-20	2020-21	2021-22	2022-23
All combined, districtwide	80,725	78,278	76,036	75,310	74,030	0	0	73,880	74,017
Retained both (2 SROs)	17,881	16,829	16,058	15,439	15,338	0	0	15,647	15,751
Partially removed (1 SRO)	13,861	13,296	12,837	12,561	12,152	0	0	12,491	12,494
Fully removed (0 SROs)	40,844	40,302	39,529	39,656	39,083	0	0	38,418	38,630
None at baseline (0 SROs)	6,406	6,656	6,956	7,179	7,338	0	0	7,324	7,142

Covariates

Student-level covariates

Free or reduced-price lunch status is used as a proxy for socioeconomic disadvantage; it is an indicator that the student was eligible for free or reduced-price lunch in the school year.

Race/ethnicity is a categorical variable with the single-value race/ethnicity group as recorded in CPS administrative records.

Gender is a categorical variable as recorded in CPS administrative records. The first year that the N (non-binary) gender code appeared in CPS administrative data transferred to the UChicago Consortium was in fall 2021–22.

English Learner (EL) status identifies whether a student was classified as an English Learner, either in the given school year (Active EL) or was previously (but was no longer) classified as an English Learner (Former EL). Students in the Never EL category were never classified as an English Learner while enrolled in CPS.

The variable **received special education services** indicates whether a student received special education services in the given school year.

The **eighth-grade GPA** variable is a student's grade point average (GPA) on the standard four-point scale in their eighth-grade year, calculated over all enrolled and graded courses. If a student repeated eighth grade, we used the latest year.

We include fixed effects for **student grade level** as a control in our difference-in-difference models.

School-level covariates

School's census block crime rate is the number of crimes reported to the Chicago Police Department in the census block where the school is located, divided by the population of the census block (from 2010). This includes both index and non-index crimes.

High schools were classified into three types for the **school type** variable: neighborhood, selective enrollment, and other citywide. Neighborhood schools are comprehensive high schools that primarily enroll students from the surrounding neighborhood. Selective enrollment high schools in Chicago are competitive and mainly have college preparation programs intended to serve high-achieving students. Other citywide schools are those that serve students citywide and often have specialized programs, such as International Baccalaureate, career and technical education, or others.

The **principal stability** variable is an indicator of whether the school's principal had been in that position in the previous school year.

The **percent of student body with economic disadvantage** is the percentage of a school's students who qualify for free or reduced-price lunch.

The **percent of student body who are Black** is the percentage of a school's students whose single-value race/ethnicity is recorded as Black/African-American.

The **percent of student body who are Latinx** is the percentage of a school's students whose single-value race/ethnicity is recorded as Latinx.

The *5Essentials* **Ambitious Instruction score** is the average of all *5Essentials* Ambitious Instruction measures for a school from 2017–18. This is considered a baseline characteristic of a school and values in other years could be directly or indirectly affected by SRO removal, so we do not use scores from other years. These scores that are averaged are on a scale of 1-99 and are a standardized and rescaled version of the precision-weighted means described earlier. The Ambitious Instruction measures include English Instruction, Math Instruction, Academic Press, and Quality of Student Discussion.[20]

The *5Essentials* **Effective Leaders score** is the average of all *5Essentials* Effective Leaders measures for a school which include Teacher Influence, Program Coherence, Teacher-Principal Trust, and Instructional Leadership and is from 2017–18.

The *5Essentials* **Collaborative Teachers score** is the average of all *5Essentials* Collaborative Teachers measures for a school which include Collaborative Practices, Collective Responsibility, School Commitment, Teacher-Teacher Trust, and Quality of Professional Development and is from 2017–18.

The *5Essentials* **Involved Families score** is the average of all *5Essentials* Involved Families measures for a school which include Parent Influence on Decision-Making, Teacher-Parent Trust, and Parent Involvement in School and is from 2017–18.

The **school 9-12 enrollment** is the total number of students enrolled in a high school in grades 9-12.

---

20 More information on score construction for the *5Essentials* Survey measures can be found in Hart et al. (2020) or at https://help.5-essentials.org/s/article/how-scores-are-calculated

Appendix B
Supplementary data displays

FIGURE B.1

SRO presence across high school students by year

SRO status in school year:

■ None at baseline (0 SROs)　■ Fully removed (0 SROs)　■ Partially removed (1 SRO)　■ Retained both (2 SROs)

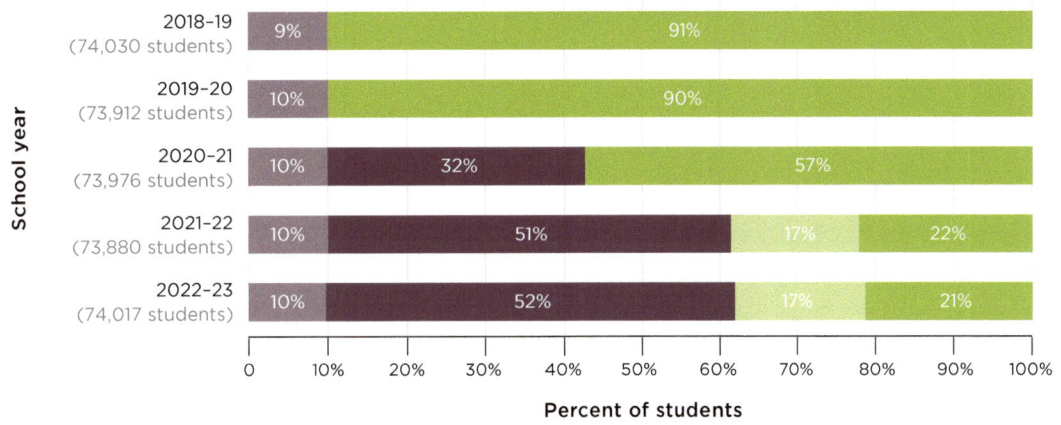

School year		
2018-19 (74,030 students)	9%	91%
2019-20 (73,912 students)	10%	90%
2020-21 (73,976 students)	10%	32%	57%
2021-22 (73,880 students)	10%	51%	17%	22%
2022-23 (74,017 students)	10%	52%	17%	21%

Percent of students

Note: Percentages within each school year may not sum to 100% due to rounding.

SRO presence by high school discipline infraction rates, 2022–23

SRO status in 2022–23:

- ■ None at baseline (0 SROs)
- ■ Fully removed (0 SROs)
- ■ Partially removed (1 SRO)
- ■ Retained both (2 SROs)

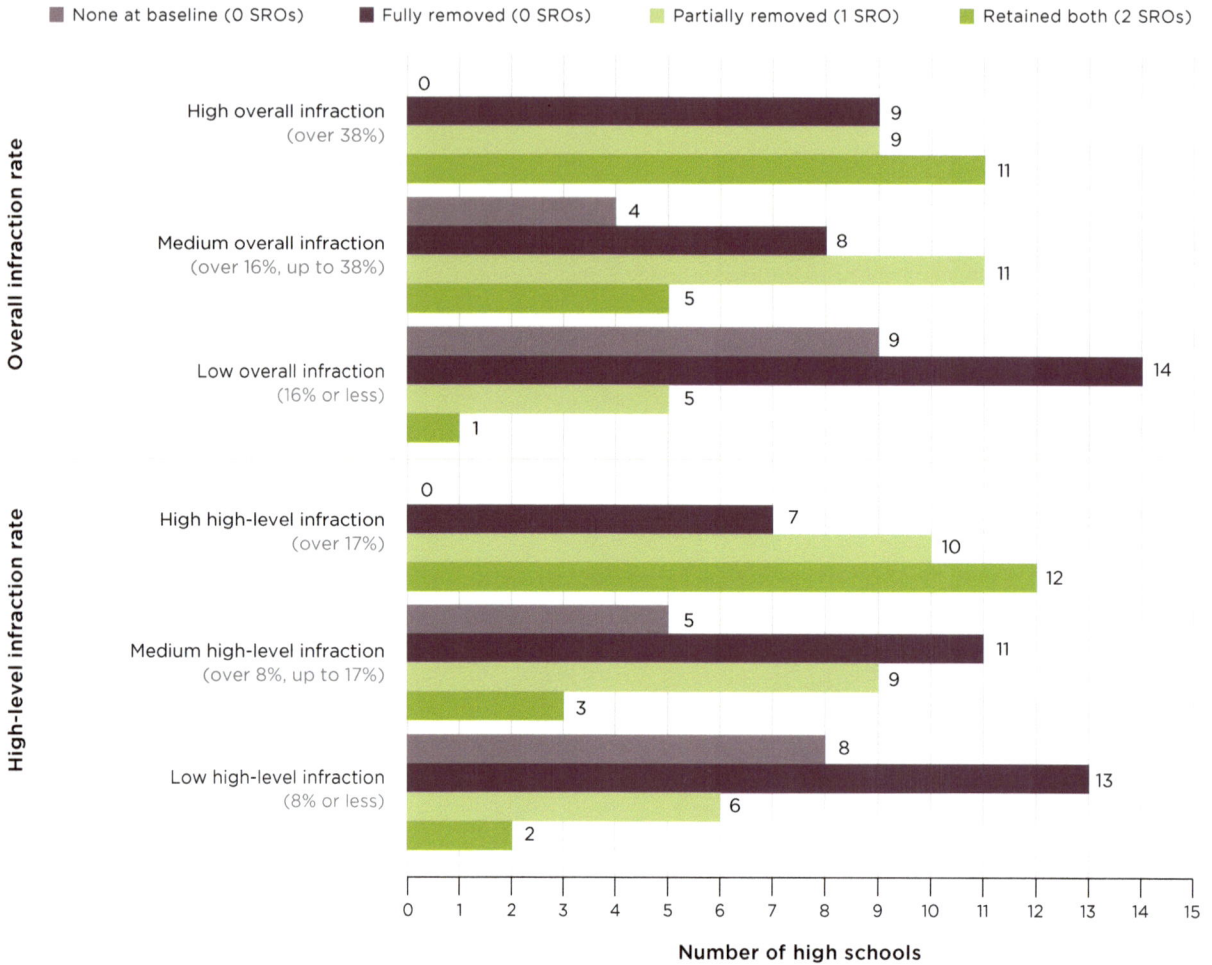

Overall infraction rate

High overall infraction (over 38%): 0, 9, 9, 11

Medium overall infraction (over 16%, up to 38%): 4, 8, 11, 5

Low overall infraction (16% or less): 9, 14, 5, 1

High-level infraction rate

High high-level infraction (over 17%): 0, 7, 10, 12

Medium high-level infraction (over 8%, up to 17%): 5, 11, 9, 3

Low high-level infraction (8% or less): 8, 13, 6, 2

Number of high schools

Note: Categories were created by dividing schools into three equal-sized groups based on the school-level percent of students with a suspension, percent of students with any infraction, and percent of students with a high-level infraction.

Appendix C
Difference-in-difference methods and estimates

We ran different models depending on whether the outcome was linear, a count, or binary and whether the unit of analysis was at the school- or student-level. Model specifications follow.

The specification for our logistic student-level models (binary outcomes: discipline infraction, high-level discipline infraction, suspension, and police notification) is provided in Equation 1.

$$\text{logit}\,(Y_{ijt}=1|\mathbf{X}_{it},\mathbf{W}_{ijt},Post_t,Partial_j,Full_j)=$$
$$\alpha+\beta_1\,(Partial_j\times Post_t)+\beta_2\,(Full_j\times Post_t)+\beta_3 Post_t+$$
$$\gamma\mathbf{X}_{it}+\delta\mathbf{W}_{ijt} \tag{1}$$

- In all equations: i indexes students, j indexes schools, and t indexes the school year (time).

- $\mathbf{X}_{it}$ is a vector of student-level characteristics for student i in year t, defined in Appendix A, which include:

  – Free or reduced-price lunch status (reference group: Not eligible)

  – Race/ethnicity (reference group: White)

  – Gender (reference group: Male)

  – English Learner (EL) status (reference group: Never EL)

  – Special education status (reference group: Did not receive services)

  – Eighth-grade GPA (note this is measured prior to year t for all students)

  – Grade level (reference group: 9th grade)

- $\mathbf{W}_{ijt}$ is a vector of indicator variables for the school (j) that student i was enrolled in during year t and δ is the vector of their coefficients. These are school fixed effects. An arbitrary school will be used as the reference category.

- $Partial_j$ and $Full_j$ indicate the treatment status of school j, whether the school partially or fully removed SROs in 2022–23, respectively. The reference group are students in schools that retained both SROs through 2022–23. There are no treatment

"main effects" in this model due to the inclusion of school fixed effects.

- $Post_t$ is an indicator that the observation is post-treatment. This takes the value of 0 for $t=0$ (2018–19) and 1 for $t=1$ (2022–23).

The specification for our linear student-level models (outcomes, student scores: Student Physical Safety, Teacher-Student Trust) is provided in Equation 2.

$$Y_{ijt}=\alpha+\beta_1\,(Partial_j\times Post_t)+\beta_2\,(Full_j\times Post_t)+$$
$$\beta_3 Post_t+\gamma\mathbf{X}_{it}+\delta\mathbf{W}_{ijt}+\varepsilon_{ijt} \tag{2}$$

All variable definitions follow from those provided for Equation 1, except that Y_{ijt} now represents a linear outcome and there is a residual term for student i in school j at time t, ε_{ijt}.

The specification for our Poisson school-level models (annual count outcomes: discipline infractions, high-level discipline infractions, suspensions, and police notifications) is provided in Equation 3.

$$\log\left(\frac{Y_{jt}|\mathbf{Z}_{jt},Post_t,Partial_j,Full_j}{Enrollment_{jt}}\right)=$$
$$\alpha+\beta_1 Partial_j\times Post_t+\beta_2 Full_j+\beta_3 Post_t+$$
$$\beta_4(Partial_j\times Post_t)+\beta_4(Full_j\times Post_t)+$$
$$\gamma\mathbf{Z}_{jt}-\log(Enrollment_{jt}) \tag{3}$$

- The exposure variable is $Enrollment_{jt}$, the number of ninth- through twelfth-grade students enrolled at school j in year t.

- $Partial_j$, $Full_j$, and $Post_j$ are defined as above for school j.

- $\mathbf{Z}_{jt}$ is a vector of school-level characteristics, defined in Appendix A, including:

  – Census block crime rate in year t

  – School type (reference category: Neighborhood; not time-varying)

  – Principal stability indicator in year t

  – Percent of student body with economic disadvantage in year t

- Percent of student body who are Black in year t
- Percent of student body who are Latinx in year t
- *5Essentials* Ambitious Instruction score in 2017–18
- *5Essentials* Effective Leaders score in 2017–18
- *5Essentials* Collaborative Teachers score in 2017–18
- *5Essentials* Involved Families score in 2017–18

We did not include the fifth essential, Supportive Environment, as the Student Physical Safety and Student-Teacher Trust measures, which are some of our outcomes, are elements of it.

The specification for our linear school-level models (outcomes, school scores: Student Physical Safety, Teacher Physical Safety, and Teacher-Student Trust) is provided in Equation 4.

$$Y_{ijt} = \alpha + \beta_1\, Partial_j + \beta_2\, Full_j + \beta_3\, Post_t +$$
$$\beta_4 (Full_j \times Post_t) + \beta_5 (Full_j \times Post_t) + \gamma \mathbf{Z}_{jt} + \varepsilon_{jt} \qquad (4)$$

All variable definitions follow from those provided for Equation 3, except that Y_{ijt} now represents a linear outcome, there is a residual term for school j at time t, ε_{jt}, and the school's total ninth- through twelfth-grade enrollment ($Enrollment_{jt}$) is now included in the $\mathbf{Z}_{jt}$ vector.

Each of the following subsections provides the model estimates for each model we ran. While difference-in-difference analyses are often used to quantify a causal effect, we do not interpret our results as causal.

First, a causal interpretation relies largely on an assumption that the outcomes have *parallel trends* in the pre-period. In this context, that would mean that the discipline and survey outcomes would need to be parallel in the years leading up to our baseline year of 2018–19. **Figures 2, 3, A.1, and A.2** in show some these trends. In addition to this visual inspection, we ran models with similar specifications to Equations 1-4 using data from 2014–15 through 2018–19 to investigate the parallel trends assumption more systematically and conditioned on our suite of control variables. Instead of the binary post variable, we included a linear time

variable that took on the values 0-4 for each of the school years 2014–15 through 2018–19, respectively. This time variable was then interacted with the treatment status variables and we conducted hypothesis testing on the coefficients of the interaction terms to test whether we have evidence against parallel trends. Because the treatment status has three levels, leading to more than one coefficient, we conducted an *F*-test or *chi2*-test as appropriate to determine whether the set of slopes on the treatment variables were significantly different from zero. The results of these significance tests are provided in each subsection below. In most cases, we obtained a *p*-value that did not provide evidence *against* the assumption, but also does not definitively provide evidence *in favor* of parallel trends. One of our chief concerns, which we cannot test largely to a lack of data (potential unobserved confounders), is the differential impact of the COVID-19 pandemic and related educational disruptions that occurred in 2019–20 and 2020–21, right as LSCs were making decisions about the SRO program in high schools in CPS. Schools that made different decisions regarding SROs may have differed in important and unobserved ways in the pandemic-affected years.

Secondly, we acknowledge nonrandom selection into treatment. The descriptive analyses in the main text described some of the ways that high schools that made different decisions about SRO presence differed. We included these variables in our difference-in-difference models. However, we do not claim that we have fully explained, by inclusion of these covariates, the selection mechanism for differing levels of SRO presence.

These are limitations on causal interpretations of the estimated differences among schools. We still believe that describing these differences, even though we cannot fully attribute them to the removal of SROs, still provides important information to CPS, the CBOs working with school communities, and the public about how schools changed after removing SROs.

Discipline infractions

Table C.1 provides the difference-in-difference estimates for the student-level discipline infraction model, specified as in Equation 1. Logistic regression is used as the outcome is binary and the estimates provided in the table are on the log odds ("logit") scale, except for the right-most column which is the odds ratio (odds for the intercept).

As described above, we conducted a *chi2*-test to determine whether the set of slopes on the treatment variables are different from zero in our pre-trends model. With a *p*-value of 0.446 [Chi2(2) = 1.615], we fail to reject the null hypothesis, meaning this does not provide evidence that the parallel trends assumption is violated at the alpha = 0.10 level.

TABLE C.1

Logistic regression output from the difference-in-difference model for the student-level discipline infraction outcome

Coefficient	Estimate	Standard error (robust)	*t*-statistic	*p*-value	Significance	Odds ratio
Difference-in-difference effects [Reference category: Retained both]						
Partial X Post	0.337	0.446	0.757	0.449		1.401
Full X Post	-0.022	0.270	-0.083	0.934		0.978
Post-treatment year (2022-23)	0.297	0.207	1.431	0.152		1.345
Qualifies for free or reduced-price lunch	0.294	0.041	7.159	<0.001	***	1.342
Student race/ethnicity [Reference category: White]						
Black	0.752	0.066	11.358	<0.001	***	2.121
Native American/ Alaskan Native	0.172	0.148	1.164	0.245		1.188
Latinx	0.112	0.040	2.844	0.004	***	1.119
Multiracial	0.211	0.104	2.025	0.043	**	1.234
Asian/Pacific Islander/ Hawaiian	-0.416	0.092	-4.507	<0.001	***	0.659
Student gender [Reference category: Male]						
Female	-0.126	0.033	-3.795	<0.001	***	0.882
Non-binary	-0.885	0.484	-1.828	0.068	*	0.413
English Learner status [Reference category: Never English Learner]						
Active English Learner	-0.166	0.038	-4.344	<0.001	***	0.847
Former English Learner	-0.245	0.037	-6.609	<0.001	***	0.783
Received special education services	-0.003	0.040	-0.067	0.946		0.997
8th-grade GPA	-0.722	0.028	-25.851	<0.001	***	0.486
Student grade level [Reference category: 9th grade]						
10th grade	-0.168	0.047	-3.549	<0.001	***	0.845
11th grade	-0.159	0.050	-3.157	0.002	***	0.853
12th grade	-0.481	0.070	-6.901	<0.001	***	0.618
Intercept	-0.130	0.161	-0.807	0.419		0.878

67 school fixed effect rows not shown

Note: For this student-level model, we used Stata's logit command with cluster robust standard errors, clustered at the campus/site. This analysis is based on 98,124 student-level observations, 49,682 in the baseline year of 2018–19 and 48,442 in 2022–23. There were 64 campus/site clusters. * indicates that differences are significant at p<0.10; ** indicates that differences are significant at p<0.05 and *** indicates that differences are significant at p<0.01.

Table C.2 provides the difference-in-difference estimates for the school-level discipline infraction model, specified as in Equation 3. Poisson regression with school enrollment as the exposure is used as the outcome is a count and the estimates provided in the table are on the log of the rate scale, except for the right-most column which is the incidence risk ratio.

As described above, we conducted a chi2-test to determine whether the set of slopes on the treatment variables are different from zero in our pre-trends model. With a p-value of 0.329 [Chi2(2) = 2.221], we fail to reject the null hypothesis, meaning this does not provide evidence that the parallel trends assumption is violated at the alpha = 0.10 level.

TABLE C.2

Poisson regression output from the difference-in-difference model for the school-level discipline infraction outcome

Coefficient	Estimate	Standard error (robust)	*t*-statistic	*p*-value	Significance	IRR
Treatment status main effects [Reference category: Retained both]						
Partial removal	-0.714	0.498	-1.433	0.152		0.490
Full removal	-1.030	0.427	-2.411	0.016	**	0.357
Post-treatment year (2022-23)	0.681	0.383	1.778	0.075	*	1.976
Difference-in-difference effects [Reference category: Retained both]						
Partial X Post	0.474	0.633	0.749	0.454		1.607
Full X Post	-0.049	0.454	-0.109	0.913		0.952
School's census block crime rate	1.234	1.038	1.188	0.235		3.434
School type [Reference category: Neighborhood]						
Selective enrollment	1.374	1.023	1.344	0.179		3.953
Other citywide	-0.632	0.381	-1.659	0.097	*	0.532
Principal stability	0.297	0.270	1.102	0.271		1.346
Percent of student body with economic disadvantage	0.028	0.028	0.999	0.318		1.029
Percent of student body who are Black	0.008	0.019	0.428	0.669		1.008
Percent of student body who are Latinx	0.012	0.019	0.626	0.532		1.012
5Essentials Ambitious Instruction score (2017–18)	-0.013	0.019	-0.676	0.499		0.987
5Essentials Effective Leaders score (2017–18)	-0.037	0.022	-1.697	0.090	*	0.964
5Essentials Collaborative Teachers score (2017–18)	0.032	0.020	1.622	0.105		1.033
5Essentials Involved Families score (2017–18)	-0.024	0.015	-1.617	0.106		0.977
Intercept	-1.302	2.037	-0.639	0.523		0.272

Note: For this school-level model, we used Stata's Poisson command with cluster robust standard errors, clustered at the campus/site, and the school's total enrollment as the exposure. This analysis is based on 142 school-level observations, 71 in the baseline year of 2018–19 and 71 in 2022–23. There were 67 campus/site clusters. * indicates that differences are significant at p<0.10; ** indicates that differences are significant at p<0.05 and *** indicates that differences are significant at p<0.01.

High-level discipline infractions

Table C.3 provides the difference-in-difference estimates for the student-level high-level discipline infraction model, specified as in Equation 1. Logistic regression is used as the outcome is binary and the estimates provided in the table are on the log odds ("logit") scale, except for the right-most column which is the odds ratio (odds for the intercept).

As described previously, we conducted a *chi2*-test to determine whether the set of slopes on the treatment variables are different from zero in our pre-trends model. With a *p*-value of 0.796 [Chi2(2) = 0.456], we fail to reject the null hypothesis, meaning this does not provide evidence that the parallel trends assumption is violated at the alpha = 0.10 level.

TABLE C.3

Logistic regression output from the difference-in-difference model for the student high-level discipline infraction outcome

Coefficient	Estimate	Standard error (robust)	*t*-statistic	*p*-value	Significance	Odds ratio
Difference-in-difference effects [Reference category: Retained both]						
Partial X Post	-0.148	0.147	-1.003	0.316		0.863
Full X Post	-0.336	0.157	-2.133	0.033	**	0.715
Post-treatment year (2022-23)	0.353	0.100	3.536	<0.001	***	1.423
Qualifies for free or reduced-price lunch	0.439	0.057	7.655	<0.001	***	1.552
Student race/ethnicity [Reference category: White]						
Black	0.992	0.103	9.646	<0.001	***	2.697
Native American/ Alaskan Native	0.309	0.224	1.377	0.169		1.362
Latinx	0.231	0.081	2.865	0.004	***	1.260
Multiracial	0.407	0.142	2.861	0.004	***	1.502
Asian/Pacific Islander/ Hawaiian	-0.404	0.117	-3.454	0.001	***	0.667
Student gender [Reference category: Male]						
Female	-0.224	0.038	-5.919	<0.001	***	0.799
Non-binary	-1.346	0.817	-1.648	0.099	*	0.260
English Learner status [Reference category: Never English Learner]						
Active English Learner	-0.310	0.051	-6.076	<0.001	***	0.734
Former English Learner	-0.387	0.043	-9.073	<0.001	***	0.679
Received special education services	0.110	0.041	2.712	0.007	***	1.117
8th-grade GPA	-0.654	0.025	-26.332	<0.001	***	0.520
Student grade level [Reference category: 9th grade]						
10th grade	-0.203	0.045	-4.486	<0.001	***	0.817
11th grade	-0.248	0.045	-5.480	<0.001	***	0.780
12th grade	-0.567	0.053	-10.742	<0.001	***	0.567
Intercept	-1.113	0.132	-8.459	<0.001	***	0.328

67 school fixed effect rows not shown

Note: For this student-level model, we used Stata's logit command with cluster robust standard errors, clustered at the campus/site. This analysis is based on 98,124 student-level observations, 49,682 in the baseline year of 2018–19 and 48,442 in 2022–23. There were 64 campus/site clusters. * indicates that differences are significant at p<0.10; ** indicates that differences are significant at p<0.05 and *** indicates that differences are significant at p<0.01.

Table **C.4** provides the difference-in-difference estimates for the school high-level discipline infraction model, specified as in Equation 3. Poisson regression with school enrollment as the exposure is used as the outcome is a count and the estimates provided in the table are on the log of the rate scale, except for the right-most column which is the incidence risk ratio.

As described previously, we conducted a *chi2*-test to determine whether the set of slopes on the treatment variables are different from zero in our pre-trends model. With a *p*-value of 0.383 [Chi2(2) = 1.919], we fail to reject the null hypothesis, meaning this does not provide evidence that the parallel trends assumption is violated at the alpha = 0.10 level.

TABLE C.4

Poisson regression output from the difference-in-difference model for the school high-level discipline infraction outcome

Coefficient	Estimate	Standard error (robust)	*t*-statistic	*p*-value	Significance	IRR
Treatment status main effects [Reference category: Retained both]						
Partial removal	0.037	0.261	0.141	0.888		1.038
Full removal	-0.017	0.186	-0.094	0.925		0.983
Post-treatment year (2022–23)	0.385	0.103	3.731	<0.001	***	1.469
Difference-in-difference effects [Reference category: Retained both]						
Partial X Post	-0.082	0.160	-0.514	0.607		0.921
Full X Post	-0.284	0.171	-1.661	0.097	*	0.752
School's census block crime rate	0.278	0.365	0.762	0.446		1.320
School type [Reference category: Neighborhood]						
Selective enrollment	-0.980	0.311	-3.146	0.002	***	0.375
Other citywide	-0.506	0.160	-3.170	0.002	***	0.603
Principal stability	-0.070	0.131	-0.534	0.594		0.932
Percent of student body with economic disadvantage	0.023	0.009	2.466	0.014	**	1.024
Percent of student body who are Black	0.009	0.006	1.434	0.152		1.009
Percent of student body who are Latinx	0.000	0.007	-0.063	0.950		1.000
5Essentials Ambitious Instruction score (2017–18)	-0.009	0.006	-1.417	0.156		0.991
5Essentials Effective Leaders score (2017–18)	0.000	0.011	0.020	0.984		1.000
5Essentials Collaborative Teachers score (2017–18)	-0.010	0.013	-0.745	0.456		0.991
5Essentials Involved Families score (2017–18)	0.007	0.009	0.767	0.443		1.007
Intercept	-3.281	0.715	-4.589	<0.001	***	0.038

Note: For this school-level model, we used Stata's Poisson command with cluster robust standard errors, clustered at the campus/site, and the school's total enrollment as the exposure. This analysis is based on 142 school-level observations, 71 in the baseline year of 2018–19 and 71 in 2022–23. There were 67 campus/site clusters. * indicates that differences are significant at p<0.10; ** indicates that differences are significant at p<0.05 and *** indicates that differences are significant at p<0.01.

Suspensions

Table C.5 provides the difference-in-difference estimates for the student-level suspension model, specified as in Equation 1. Logistic regression is used as the outcome is binary and the estimates provided in the table are on the log odds ("logit") scale, except for the right-most column which is the odds ratio (odds for the intercept).

As described previously, we conducted a *chi2*-test to determine whether the set of slopes on the treatment variables are different from zero in our pre-trends model. With a *p*-value of 0.253 [Chi2(2) = 2.752], we fail to reject the null hypothesis, meaning this does not provide evidence that the parallel trends assumption is violated at the alpha = 0.10 level.

Logistic regression output from the difference-in-difference model for the student-level suspension outcome

Coefficient	Estimate	Standard error (robust)	*t*-statistic	*p*-value	Significance	Odds ratio
Difference-in-difference effects [Reference category: Retained both]						
Partial X Post	-0.224	0.326	-0.686	0.492		0.799
Full X Post	-0.054	0.282	-0.193	0.847		0.947
Post-treatment year (2022–23)	-0.135	0.239	-0.566	0.572		0.874
Qualifies for free or reduced-price lunch	0.427	0.060	7.103	<0.001	***	1.533
Student race/ethnicity [Reference category: White]						
Black	0.991	0.076	13.015	<0.001	***	2.695
Native American/ Alaskan Native	0.319	0.188	1.696	0.090	*	1.375
Latinx	0.235	0.062	3.784	<0.001	***	1.265
Multiracial	0.406	0.150	2.712	0.007	***	1.501
Asian/Pacific Islander/ Hawaiian	-0.429	0.123	-3.501	<0.001	***	0.651
Student gender [Reference category: Male]						
Female	-0.162	0.036	-4.437	<0.001	***	0.851
Non-binary	-1.295	0.868	-1.492	0.136		0.274
English Learner status [Reference category: Never English Learner]						
Active English Learner	-0.205	0.045	-4.497	<0.001	***	0.815
Former English Learner	-0.353	0.044	-8.004	<0.001	***	0.703
Received special education services	0.052	0.042	1.258	0.208		1.054
8th-grade GPA	-0.701	0.030	-23.098	<0.001	***	0.496
Student grade level [Reference category: 9th grade]						
10th grade	-0.108	0.050	-2.180	0.029	**	0.898
11th grade	-0.167	0.058	-2.885	0.004	***	0.846
12th grade	-0.573	0.070	-8.143	<0.001	***	0.564
Intercept	-0.761	0.154	-4.944	<0.001	***	0.467

67 school fixed effect rows not shown

Note: For this student-level model, we used Stata's logit command with cluster robust standard errors, clustered at the campus/site. This analysis is based on 98,124 student-level observations, 49,682 in the baseline year of 2018–19 and 48,442 in 2022–23. There were 64 campus/site clusters. * indicates that differences are significant at p<0.10; ** indicates that differences are significant at p<0.05 and *** indicates that differences are significant at p<0.01.

Table **C.6** provides the difference-in-difference estimates for the school-level suspension model, specified as in Equation 3. Poisson regression with school enrollment as the exposure is used as the outcome is a count and the estimates provided in the table are on the log of the rate scale, except for the right-most column which is the incidence risk ratio.

As described previously, we conducted a *chi2*-test to determine whether the set of slopes on the treatment variables are different from zero in our pre-trends model. With a *p*-value of 0.570 [Chi2(2) = 1.122], we fail to reject the null hypothesis, meaning this does not provide evidence that the parallel trends assumption is violated at the alpha = 0.10 level.

TABLE C.6

Poisson regression output from the difference-in-difference model for the school-level suspension outcome

Coefficient	Estimate	Standard error (robust)	*t*-statistic	*p*-value	Significance	IRR
Treatment status main effects [Reference category: Retained both]						
Partial removal	-0.514	0.415	-1.239	0.215		0.598
Full removal	-0.521	0.514	-1.013	0.311		0.594
Post-treatment year (2022–23)	-0.372	0.230	-1.622	0.105		0.689
Difference-in-difference effects [Reference category: Retained both]						
Partial X Post	0.051	0.308	0.164	0.869		1.052
Full X Post	0.167	0.368	0.455	0.649		1.182
School's census block crime rate	-0.263	0.656	-0.401	0.688		0.769
School type [Reference category: Neighborhood]						
Selective enrollment	-1.595	0.416	-3.830	<0.001	***	0.203
Other citywide	-0.671	0.356	-1.885	0.059	*	0.511
Principal stability	-0.010	0.227	-0.042	0.966		0.991
Percent of student body with economic disadvantage	0.021	0.015	1.410	0.158		1.021
Percent of student body who are Black	0.016	0.010	1.651	0.099	*	1.017
Percent of student body who are Latinx	0.010	0.011	0.866	0.386		1.010
5Essentials Ambitious Instruction score (2017–18)	0.012	0.014	0.851	0.395		1.012
5Essentials Effective Leaders score (2017–18)	0.007	0.016	0.436	0.663		1.007
5Essentials Collaborative Teachers score (2017–18)	0.002	0.018	0.126	0.900		1.002
5Essentials Involved Families score (2017–18)	-0.019	0.017	-1.137	0.255		0.981
Intercept	-3.779	1.247	-3.031	0.002	***	0.023

Note: For this school-level model, we used Stata's Poisson command with cluster robust standard errors, clustered at the campus/site, and the school's total enrollment as the exposure. This analysis is based on 142 school-level observations, 71 in the baseline year of 2018–19 and 71 in 2022–23. There were 67 campus/site clusters. * indicates that differences are significant at p<0.10; ** indicates that differences are significant at p<0.05 and *** indicates that differences are significant at p<0.01.

Police notifications

Table C.7 provides the difference-in-difference estimates for the student-level police notification model, specified as in Equation 1. Logistic regression is used as the outcome is binary and the estimates provided in the table are on the log odds ("logit") scale, except for the rightmost column which is the odds ratio (odds for the intercept).

As described previously, we conducted a *chi2*-test to determine whether the set of slopes on the treatment variables are different from zero in our pre-trends model. With a *p*-value of 0.075 [Chi2(2) = 5.182], we reject the null hypothesis, meaning we have evidence to conclude that the parallel trends assumption is violated at the alpha = 0.10 level.

TABLE C.7

Logistic regression output from the difference-in-difference model for the student-level police notification outcome

Coefficient	Estimate	Standard error (robust)	*t*-statistic	*p*-value	Significance	Odds ratio
Difference-in-difference effects [Reference category: Retained both]						
Partial X Post	0.016	0.428	0.038	0.969		1.017
Full X Post	-0.444	0.476	-0.933	0.351		0.642
Post-treatment year (2022–23)	0.047	0.276	0.169	0.866		1.048
Qualifies for free or reduced-price lunch	0.742	0.133	5.571	<0.001	***	2.100
Student race/ethnicity [Reference category: White]						
Black	1.142	0.254	4.492	<0.001	***	3.133
Native American/ Alaskan Native	1.324	0.388	3.413	0.001	***	3.757
Latinx	0.368	0.184	1.996	0.046	**	1.444
Multiracial	0.371	0.432	0.860	0.390		1.450
Asian/Pacific Islander/ Hawaiian	-0.352	0.352	-1.001	0.317		0.703
Student gender [Reference category: Male]						
Female	-0.169	0.108	-1.561	0.119		0.845
English Learner status [Reference category: Never English Learner]						
Active English Learner	-0.663	0.131	-5.057	<0.001	***	0.515
Former English Learner	-0.497	0.095	-5.257	<0.001	***	0.608
Received special education services	0.213	0.074	2.878	0.004	***	1.238
8th-grade GPA	-0.654	0.061	-10.643	<0.001	***	0.520
Student grade level [Reference category: 9th grade]						
10th grade	-0.211	0.124	-1.698	0.090	*	0.810
11th grade	-0.284	0.120	-2.361	0.018	**	0.753
12th grade	-0.507	0.142	-3.574	<0.001	***	0.602
Intercept	-2.984	0.421	-7.087	<0.001	***	0.051

67 school fixed effect rows not shown

Note: For this student-level model, we used Stata's logit command with cluster robust standard errors, clustered at the campus/site. This analysis is based on 98,054 student-level observations, 49,682 in the baseline year of 2018-19 and 48,442 in 2022-23. Seventy students with a gender value of non-binary were excluded due to no variation in outcome. There were 64 campus/site clusters. * indicates that differences are significant at p<0.10; ** indicates that differences are significant at p<0.05 and *** indicates that differences are significant at p<0.01.

Table **C.8** provides the difference-in-difference estimates for the school-level police notification model, specified as in Equation 3. Poisson regression with school enrollment as the exposure is used as the outcome is a count and the estimates provided in the table are on the log of the rate scale, except for the right-most column which is the incidence risk ratio.

As described previously, we conducted a *chi2*-test to determine whether the set of slopes on the treatment variables are different from zero in our pre-trends model. With a *p*-value of 0.343 [Chi2(2) = 2.138], we fail to reject the null hypothesis, meaning this does not provide evidence that the parallel trends assumption is violated at the alpha = 0.10 level.

TABLE C.8

Poisson regression output from the difference-in-difference model the school-level police notification outcome

Coefficient	Estimate	Standard error (robust)	*t*-statistic	*p*-value	Significance	IRR
Treatment status main effects [Reference category: Retained both]						
Partial removal	0.188	0.411	0.457	0.648		1.206
Full removal	0.146	0.471	0.310	0.757		1.157
Post-treatment year (2022–23)	0.115	0.266	0.431	0.666		1.122
Difference-in-difference effects [Reference category: Retained both]						
Partial X Post	-0.126	0.438	-0.288	0.774		0.882
Full X Post	-0.637	0.586	-1.086	0.277		0.529
School's census block crime rate	1.760	1.143	1.540	0.124		5.814
School type [Reference category: Neighborhood]						
Selective enrollment	-1.743	0.760	-2.292	0.022	**	0.175
Other citywide	-0.961	0.470	-2.045	0.041	**	0.383
Principal stability	0.025	0.252	0.100	0.921		1.025
Percent of student body with economic disadvantage	0.030	0.022	1.323	0.186		1.030
Percent of student body who are Black	-0.005	0.015	-0.297	0.766		0.995
Percent of student body who are Latinx	-0.011	0.019	-0.590	0.556		0.989
5Essentials Ambitious Instruction score (2017–18)	0.002	0.014	0.117	0.907		1.002
5Essentials Effective Leaders score (2017–18)	0.010	0.019	0.516	0.606		1.010
5Essentials Collaborative Teachers score (2017–18)	-0.019	0.020	-0.956	0.339		0.981
5Essentials Involved Families score (2017–18)	-0.011	0.027	-0.402	0.688		0.989
Intercept	-4.846	1.599	-3.030	0.002	***	0.008

Note: For this school-level model, we used Stata's Poisson command with cluster robust standard errors, clustered at the campus/site, and the school's total enrollment as the exposure. This analysis is based on 142 school-level observations, 71 in the baseline year of 2018–19 and 71 in 2022–23. There were 67 campus/site clusters. * indicates that differences are significant at p<0.10; ** indicates that differences are significant at p<0.05 and *** indicates that differences are significant at p<0.01.

Student Physical Safety

Table C.9 provides the difference-in-difference estimates for the student-level Student Physical Safety model, specified as in Equation 2.

As described above, we conducted an F-test to determine whether the set of slopes on the treatment variables are different from zero in our pre-trends model. With a p-value of 0.265 [$F(1, 67) = 1.262$], we fail to reject the null hypothesis, meaning this does not provide evidence that the parallel trends assumption is violated, at the alpha = 0.10 level.

TABLE C.9

Linear regression output from the difference-in-difference model for the Student Physical Safety student-level outcome

Coefficient	Estimate	Standard error (robust)	t-statistic	p-value	Significance
Difference-in-difference effects [Reference category: Retained both]					
Partial X Post	0.100	0.179	0.560	0.578	
Full X Post	0.120	0.170	0.702	0.485	
Post-treatment year (2022–23)	-0.443	0.157	-2.826	0.006	***
Qualifies for free or reduced-price lunch	-0.142	0.035	-4.108	<0.001	***
Student race/ethnicity [Reference category: White]					
Black	-0.167	0.093	-1.802	0.076	*
Native American/Alaskan Native	-0.210	0.165	-1.270	0.209	
Latinx	-0.226	0.069	-3.256	0.002	***
Multiracial	-0.080	0.077	-1.040	0.302	
Asian/Pacific Islander/Hawaiian	-0.406	0.075	-5.447	<0.001	***
Student gender [Reference category: Male]					
Female	-0.289	0.023	-12.739	<0.001	***
Non-binary	-1.246	0.291	-4.282	<0.001	***
English Learner status [Reference category: Never English Learner]					
Active English Learner	-0.050	0.032	-1.571	0.121	
Former English Learner	0.003	0.027	0.128	0.899	
Received special education services	-0.027	0.024	-1.131	0.262	
8th-grade GPA	0.061	0.021	2.912	0.005	***
Student grade level [Reference category: 9th grade]					
10th grade	-0.013	0.023	-0.573	0.569	
11th grade	0.003	0.030	0.089	0.930	
12th grade	0.117	0.024	4.984	<0.001	***
Intercept	1.394	0.125	11.129	<0.001	***
67 school fixed effect rows not shown					

Note: For this student-level model, we used Stata's regress command with cluster robust standard errors, clustered at the campus/site. This analysis is based on 66,043 student-level observations, 37,025 in the baseline year of 2018–19 and 29,018 in 2022–23. There were 64 campus/site clusters. * indicates that differences are significant at p<0.10; ** indicates that differences are significant at p<0.05 and *** indicates that differences are significant at p<0.01.

Table **C.10** provides the difference-in-difference estimates for the school-level Student Physical Safety model, specified as in Equation 4.

As described previously, we conducted an *F*-test to determine whether the set of slopes on the treatment variables are different from zero in our pre-trends model. With a *p*-value of 0.402 [F(1, 66) = 0.712], we fail to reject the null hypothesis, meaning this does not provide evidence that the parallel trends assumption is violated at the alpha = 0.10 level.

TABLE C.10

Linear regression output from the difference-in-difference model for the Student Physical Safety school-level outcome

Coefficient	Estimate	Standard error (robust)	*t*-statistic	*p*-value	Significance
Treatment status main effects [Reference category: Retained both]					
Partial removal	-0.044	0.091	-0.488	0.627	
Full removal	0.111	0.080	1.397	0.167	
Post-treatment year (2022–23)	-0.399	0.108	-3.677	<0.001	***
Difference-in-difference effects [Reference category: Retained both]					
Partial X Post	0.094	0.122	0.771	0.443	
Full X Post	0.059	0.125	0.475	0.636	
School's census block crime rate	-0.646	0.229	-2.821	0.006	***
School type [Reference category: Neighborhood]					
Selective enrollment	0.221	0.073	3.046	0.003	***
Other citywide	0.191	0.051	3.780	<0.001	***
Principal stability	0.086	0.056	1.521	0.133	
Percent of student body with economic disadvantage	-0.014	0.003	-4.741	<0.001	***
Percent of student body who are Black	0.003	0.002	1.279	0.206	
Percent of student body who are Latinx	0.001	0.002	0.674	0.503	
5Essentials Ambitious Instruction score (2017–18)	0.003	0.002	1.454	0.151	
5Essentials Effective Leaders score (2017–18)	0.005	0.003	1.812	0.074	*
5Essentials Collaborative Teachers score (2017–18)	0.004	0.003	1.219	0.227	
5Essentials Involved Families score (2017–18)	-0.002	0.003	-0.714	0.478	
School 9-12 enrollment	0.000	0.000	-1.279	0.205	
Intercept	1.270	0.225	5.652	<0.001	***

Note: For this school-level model, we used Stata's regress command with cluster robust standard errors, clustered at the campus/site. This analysis is based on 142 school-level observations, 71 in the baseline year of 2018–19 and 71 in 2022–23. There were 67 campus/site clusters. * indicates that differences are significant at p<0.10; ** indicates that differences are significant at p<0.05 and *** indicates that differences are significant at p<0.01.

Teacher Physical Safety

Table C.11 provides the difference-in-difference estimates for the school-level Teacher Physical Safety model, specified as in Equation 4. There is no student-level model for this outcome as the items are not answered by students.

As described previously, we conducted an *F*-test to determine whether the set of slopes on the treatment variables are different from zero in our pre-trends model. With a *p*-value of 0.997 [F(1, 66) < 0.001], we fail to reject the null hypothesis, meaning this does not provide evidence that the parallel trends assumption is violated at the alpha = 0.10 level.

TABLE C.11

Linear regression output from the difference-in-difference model for the Teacher Physical Safety school-level outcome

Coefficient	Estimate	Standard error (robust)	*t*-statistic	*p*-value	Significance
Treatment status main effects [Reference category: Retained both]					
Partial removal	0.352	0.253	1.391	0.169	
Full removal	0.324	0.213	1.520	0.133	
Post-treatment year (2022–23)	-0.385	0.279	-1.378	0.173	
Difference-in-difference effects [Reference category: Retained both]					
Partial X Post	-0.117	0.365	-0.322	0.749	
Full X Post	-0.161	0.360	-0.448	0.656	
School's census block crime rate	-1.811	0.621	-2.917	0.005	***
School type [Reference category: Neighborhood]					
Selective enrollment	1.452	0.315	4.609	<0.001	***
Other citywide	0.690	0.226	3.056	0.003	***
Principal stability	0.443	0.180	2.468	0.016	**
Percent of student body with economic disadvantage	-0.055	0.013	-4.370	<0.001	***
Percent of student body who are Black	0.017	0.009	1.937	0.057	*
Percent of student body who are Latinx	0.023	0.009	2.517	0.014	**
5Essentials Ambitious Instruction score (2017–18)	0.002	0.010	0.172	0.864	
5Essentials Effective Leaders score (2017–18)	0.007	0.011	0.614	0.541	
5Essentials Collaborative Teachers score (2017–18)	0.026	0.015	1.807	0.075	*
5Essentials Involved Families score (2017–18)	0.003	0.012	0.283	0.778	
School 9-12 enrollment	0.000	0.000	-2.828	0.006	***
Intercept	1.210	0.766	1.578	0.119	

Note: For this school-level model, we used Stata's regress command with cluster robust standard errors, clustered at the campus/site. This analysis is based on 142 school-level observations, 71 in the baseline year of 2018-19 and 71 in 2022–23. There were 67 campus/site clusters. * indicates that differences are significant at p<0.10; ** indicates that differences are significant at p<0.05 and *** indicates that differences are significant at p<0.01.

Student-Teacher Trust

Table C.12 provides the difference-in-difference estimates for the student-level Student-Teacher Trust model, specified as in Equation 2.

As described previously, we conducted an *F*-test to determine whether the set of slopes on the treatment variables are different from zero in our pre-trends model. With a *p*-value of 0.114 [$F(1, 67)$ = 2.571], we fail to reject the null hypothesis, meaning this does not provide evidence that the parallel trends assumption is violated, at the alpha = 0.10 level.

TABLE C.12

Linear regression output from the difference-in-difference model for the Student-Teacher Trust student-level outcome

Coefficient	Estimate	Standard error (robust)	*t*-statistic	*p*-value	Significance
Difference-in-difference effects [Reference category: Retained both]					
Partial X Post	-0.048	0.102	-0.471	0.639	
Full X Post	-0.006	0.093	-0.064	0.949	
Post-treatment year (2022–23)	0.008	0.076	0.100	0.921	
Qualifies for free or reduced-price lunch	0.032	0.023	1.380	0.173	
Student race/ethnicity [Reference category: White]					
Black	-0.115	0.028	-4.062	<0.001	***
Native American/Alaskan Native	-0.016	0.125	-0.127	0.899	
Latinx	-0.051	0.016	-3.164	0.002	***
Multiracial	-0.148	0.060	-2.464	0.016	**
Asian/Pacific Islander/Hawaiian	-0.015	0.057	-0.256	0.799	
Student gender [Reference category: Male]					
Female	-0.200	0.032	-6.312	<0.001	***
Non-binary	-0.338	0.235	-1.439	0.155	
English Learner status [Reference category: Never English Learner]					
Active English Learner	0.153	0.018	8.453	<0.001	***
Former English Learner	0.103	0.022	4.732	<0.001	***
Received special education services	0.090	0.037	2.447	0.017	**
8th-grade GPA	0.282	0.023	12.123	<0.001	***
Student grade level [Reference category: 9th grade]					
10th grade	-0.068	0.025	-2.686	0.009	***
11th grade	-0.075	0.059	-1.257	0.213	
12th grade	0.112	0.034	3.282	0.002	***
Intercept	0.479	0.062	7.730	<0.001	***

67 school fixed effect rows not shown

Note: For this student-level model, we used Stata's regress command with cluster robust standard errors, clustered at the campus/site. This analysis is based on 66,043 student-level observations, 37,025 in the baseline year of 2018–19 and 29,018 in 2022–23. There were 64 campus/site clusters. * indicates that differences are significant at p<0.10; ** indicates that differences are significant at p<0.05 and *** indicates that differences are significant at p<0.01.

Table C.13 provides the difference-in-difference estimates for the school-level Student-Teacher Trust model, specified as in Equation 4.

As described above, we conducted an F-test to determine whether the set of slopes on the treatment variables are different from zero in our pre-trends model. With a p-value of 0.696 [$F(1, 66) = 0.154$], we fail to reject the null hypothesis, meaning this does not provide evidence that the parallel trends assumption is violated at the alpha = 0.10 level.

TABLE C.13

Linear regression output from the difference-in-difference model for the Student-Teacher Trust school-level outcome

Coefficient	Estimate	Standard error (robust)	t-statistic	p-value	Significance
Treatment status main effects [Reference category: Retained both]					
Partial removal	0.042	0.074	0.575	0.567	
Full removal	0.069	0.067	1.031	0.306	
Post-treatment year (2022–23)	-0.072	0.072	-0.996	0.323	
Difference-in-difference effects [Reference category: Retained both]					
Partial X Post	-0.022	0.087	-0.248	0.805	
Full X Post	0.033	0.084	0.397	0.693	
School's census block crime rate	-0.349	0.156	-2.231	0.029	**
School type [Reference category: Neighborhood]					
Selective enrollment	0.130	0.064	2.031	0.046	**
Other citywide	0.051	0.050	1.008	0.317	
Principal stability	0.066	0.038	1.742	0.086	*
Percent of student body with economic disadvantage	0.000	0.002	0.008	0.994	
Percent of student body who are Black	-0.002	0.001	-1.437	0.155	
Percent of student body who are Latinx	0.000	0.001	-0.323	0.748	
5Essentials Ambitious Instruction score (2017–18)	0.005	0.002	3.100	0.003	***
5Essentials Effective Leaders score (2017–18)	0.002	0.002	1.104	0.274	
5Essentials Collaborative Teachers score (2017–18)	0.002	0.003	0.568	0.572	
5Essentials Involved Families score (2017–18)	-0.001	0.002	-0.466	0.643	
School 9-12 enrollment	0.000	0.000	-0.551	0.584	
Intercept	0.395	0.185	2.135	0.036	**

Note: For this school-level model, we used Stata's regress command with cluster robust standard errors, clustered at the campus/site. This analysis is based on 142 school-level observations, 71 in the baseline year of 2018-19 and 71 in 2022-23. There were 67 campus/site clusters. * indicates that differences are significant at $p<0.10$; ** indicates that differences are significant at $p<0.05$ and *** indicates that differences are significant at $p<0.01$.

ABOUT THE AUTHORS

AMY ARNESON is a Senior Research Associate at the UChicago Consortium, leading and supporting mixed-methods research projects with advanced quantitative analysis, visualization, and modeling. Amy focuses on conducting rigorous, meaningful, and timely research and, importantly, making the results accessible so that they can be used by educators to improve college and career outcomes for public high school students. Her work is situated in two main areas: college and career readiness and school climate. She applies her methodological expertise to examinations of secondary, post-secondary, and workforce transitions with a focus on the outcomes of career and technical education programs in high schools and community colleges. Additionally, she examines the policies that support positive perceptions of school climate for both students and adults working in schools. Amy has worked in the education field for 15 years, first as a high school math and statistics teacher. She is an alumna of the Center for Education Policy Research at Harvard University's Strategic Data Project and earned her PhD in education from the University of California, Berkeley.

REBECCA HINZE-PIFER is an Assistant Professor in Education Policy, Organization, and Leadership at the University of Illinois Urbana-Champaign. Rebecca's research focuses on school-based approaches to reducing social inequality, with particular focus on programs and practices influencing adolescent socioemotional development. Her work includes randomized field experiments of school-based programs and quasi-experimental studies using school administrative data to understand the impacts of school policies. Rebecca has published and presented on a range of related topics, including school discipline, teacher classroom management practices, and student responses to community violence. Rebecca was a public school teacher for seven years before earning her master's degree in public policy from George Washington University and her PhD in public policy from the University of Chicago.

KAITLYN FRANKLIN is a Research Analyst at the UChicago Consortium, providing data and analytic support across Consortium projects by cleaning and building large-scale databases. She is currently working to identify key indicators of student success and academic attainment for English Learners in Chicago Public Schools. Before joining the UChicago Consortium, Kaitlyn served as the Education Policy Intern for Clarke County School District in Athens, Georgia. There, she designed, wrote, and implemented monthly policy briefings and overhauled the district's policy organization system to streamline the policy review process. Kaitlyn is passionate about working toward more equitable opportunities and outcomes for students in the public school system

DAVID W. JOHNSON is a Research Assistant Professor at the Center for Childhood Resilience in the Pritzker Department of Psychiatry and Behavioral Health at Lurie Children's Hospital. David's research focuses broadly on how school and classroom contexts affect the mental and behavioral health and wellness of young people, as well as their academic achievement and attainment. David's research explores the contexts and experiences that contribute to how both children and adults learn. Prior projects include efforts to describe and understand the noncognitive factors that shape students' academic success, as well as the creation of a developmental framework for understanding young adult success inside and beyond school. David has also been closely involved in the planning and facilitation of a national network of school support organizations and school districts aimed at creating more equitable learning environments for historically marginalized and oppressed children and communities. His past and current work reflect a thoroughgoing commitment to building the capacity of educators to create developmentally rich learning experiences for all children, particularly across lines of racial, class, and cultural difference. David is a former Washington, DC Public Schools teacher and holds master's degrees in social service administration and divinity, and a doctorate in social service administration from the University of Chicago Crown Family School of Social Work, Practice, and Policy.

Steering Committee

GREG JONES
Co-Chair
The Academy Group

CARLA RUBALCAVA
Co-Chair
Mikva Challenge

Institutional Members

BOGDANA CHKOUMBOVA
Chicago Public Schools

STACY DAVIS GATES
Chicago Teachers Union

SARAH DICKSON
Chicago Public Schools

JASON HELFER
Illinois State Board of Education

SHANNAE JACKSON
Chicago Public Schools

TROY LARAVIERE
Chicago Principals and
Administrators Association

Individual Members

MARIANA BARRAGAN TORRES
Illinois Workforce and Education
Research Collaborative (IWERC)

EURYDICE BEVLY
Carnegie Elementary and
Roosevelt University

NANCY CHAVEZ
Slalom

SHARON COLEMAN
Mount Vernon Elementary School

MARSHALL HATCH
The Maafa Redemption Project

MEGAN HOUGARD
Chicago Public Schools

BRIAN KELLY
Dr. Martin Luther King Jr.
College Prep

PRANAV KOTHARI
Revolution Impact, LLC

AMANDA LEWIS
University of Illinois at Chicago

LUISIANA MELENDEZ
Erikson Institute

SHAZIA MILLER
Mathematica

KAFI MORAGNE-PATTERSON
Chicago Urban League

NATALIE NERIS
Education Consultant

TALI RAVIV
Center for Childhood Resilience at
Ann & Robert H. Lurie Children's
Hospital of Chicago

ELLEN SCHUMER
COFI

REBECCA VONDERLACK-NAVARRO
Latino Policy Forum

ACASIA WILSON FEINBERG
Wilson Feinberg Consultants, LLC

JOHN ZEIGLER
DePaul University

www.ingramcontent.com/pod-product-compliance
Lightning Source LLC
Chambersburg PA
CBHW060856270326
41934CB00003B/170